Daring Destiny

by

Emma Dell

Daring Destiny

Copyright 2006
by
Emma Dell
Cover design by Renny James
Cover photo by Winker
ISBN 1-932196-79-X

Special Delivery Books
WordWright Business Park
46561 SH 118
Alpine, TX 79830

Printed in the United States of America

To my mother,
Mary Troyer Schwartz
and
my daughters,
Marilynn and Brooke,
with Love

Introduction

Growing up in a strict Amish family with seven brothers and two sisters, gave me a solid foundation in life which has helped me to survive. I truly cherish my upbringing and love and respect my family. There are rules in the Amish church that do not make sense to me, and that is why I chose to strike out to find a life that suits me better.

I've written this story about my transition into the "English" world, to the best of my memory.

Emma Dell

Chapter 1

Family Life

On that cold day, December 3, 1960, my sister Lydia bundled us little kids up in heavy coats and mittens and took us down the hill to Grandma's house. I didn't know why, but felt something wasn't right. Mom seemed kind of funny and Dad acted nervous. He moved their bed out into the living room next to the wood stove to, "Keep Mom warm," he said.

Now I stood with my nose up against Grandma's window watching the house when I saw a car pull into the driveway. A tall man in a long, black coat and hat came walking toward the house, carrying a large black bag of some sort. He knocked on the door and someone let him inside.

This whole thing, so out of the ordinary, piqued my curiosity, so I asked my Grandma about it.

She only said, "Emmy, you have to be patient, just wait and see."

At two-and-a-half, I didn't understand the concept of patience, but tried to do as she asked, and sat quietly by the window watching the house.

After a couple of hours, Lydia came down to Grandma's house with a big announcement. "We have a new baby brother!"

She reached for my hand and led me home. I wanted to see my new little brother.

There, on the bed in the living room, Mom lay with the new baby in her arms.

"Emmy, come and see," she said softly.

Tentatively I stepped closer while Mom pushed aside the blanket. I gasped in wonder at the little face, the perfect little hands and feet, the little whimpering noises.

"His name is Joseph, but I think we should call him Seppy. What do you think of him?"

Honestly, I didn't know what to think of him. I only knew he'd take all of my mother's time away from me. He'd even get to sleep with Mom and Dad, which made me very unhappy. I felt as though this little squirmy thing had taken my place in my parents' hearts. Then I figured maybe he'd be someone to play with when he got old enough, so maybe it wouldn't bother me so much anymore.

ೞೞೞ

Our house, built into a hill, featured a stairway of huge rocks that Mom made off-limits to us. Mom let Ben, Seppy, and me play in the front yard while she worked in the washhouse. Seppy couldn't understand the idea of "off limits," so Mom put our family dog, Shep, at the top of the stairway to keep us away from it. When Seppy crawled to the stairway Shep nudged him with his nose and tried to turn him around. When Seppy showed determination, Shep picked him up by his clothing at the back of his neck and dragged him back to where he could play!

I enjoyed watching clever Shep, and we all loved him. He had long red hair and brown eyes with a pointed face. I don't know his breed, but we all recognized him as part of our large family of seven boys and three girls, with John as the oldest of our brood.

Shep could do anything. He herded the cattle almost every day. If they got within sight in the pasture, he'd run in by himself to drive them up to the gate. If the cows roamed deeper into the pasture, one of my brothers walked with Shep to round them up.

When he got old, Mom started looking for a puppy. She found an ad in *The Grit*, for an English Shepherd puppy, and wrote to the address listed. When the people answered her letter, she found out the puppy was solid black with a tiny white spot on her chest and on the tip of her tail. Mom liked that description and hired our neighbor to drive her to Harrisburg, Pennsylvania, forty miles from our home in tiny Meiserville.

Mom paid twenty-five dollars for that little dog and returned home with a fluffy black, squirming puppy that we named Cassy after the black lady in *Uncle Tom's Cabin*.

When Cassy turned about a year old, Shep died. Cassy had some awesome shoes to fill because Shep ranked as the best dog in the world. Cassy didn't have a problem taking over because she had excellent training.

CB CB CB

At mealtime, the boys sat on the bench behind the table

and around the end. Dad sat at the head and Mom next to him. With John as the oldest, followed by Peter (Pete), Lydia, Mose (Buop), Fannie (Franie), Chris, Jerry (Yarm), Ben, me, and Joseph (Seppy), we filled up that kitchen at every mealtime.

As a young girl I realized that our family lived differently than most everyone else I knew about, and began to ask Mom questions about this.

She said, "Emmy, the world is a very bad place, so we keep ourselves separate because that's where the devil lives."

Her answer saddened me because I had made friends with the neighbor children, and we occasionally played together. I didn't think of them as bad, but if Mom said so, I surely had to believe it.

I was almost four years old when my oldest brother John, then twenty, came home for a visit. John had decided at seventeen that he didn't want to continue his life in the Amish church and left home. I couldn't wait to see him, and when he walked in the door, I thought him so tall and handsome.

"There you are, Emmy!" he shouted when he saw me. He picked me up and tossed me into the air and caught me.

I laughed so hard, my sides hurt. I loved that he came home, but apparently Mom and Dad didn't feel the same.

They seemed angry with him, raised their voices and said things like, "You're living a sinful life! Unless you repent, come home and come back to the Amish Church, you'll have no place in heaven. You'll end up in hell for all eternity!"

The thought of my big brother in hell upset me so

much. I felt so proud of John and didn't think he'd done anything bad.

When I had a moment alone with my mother I asked her, "Why are you and Dad so angry with John?"

She took my hand in hers and very gently said, "He didn't obey his parents and therefore he didn't obey the Lord."

That answer only made me feel sad for John and angry with God and my parents, but that was something I kept to myself.

೮೮೮

In September 1964, I was six-years-old, and I prepared to go to school. How exciting for me! Our farm sat across the creek from the town and overlooked the whole valley. I thought it quite beautiful especially in the fall when the leaves turned bright yellow and red.

We had some oak trees that turned a really deep, dark red color. Mom, a creative soul, asked me to walk up the hill with her on a beautiful fall day. We went way up to the top of the hill that overlooked Meiserville and she sat with paper and crayons and drew a picture of the little town with all the pretty fall colors.

Our home almost operated like a little town in itself. We had the main house with a full basement and ground cellar, two floors above this, and a big attic. We also owned a second house, smaller, down the hill about one hundred feet. The springhouse sat beneath it where a little spring came up from the ground. That spring ran constantly, and felt cold even in the summer, and always tasted so good.

Grandma and Grandpa lived in the small house. Below them sat the chicken house and other outbuildings, a barn, pig shed, implement shed, another big barn where we kept the feed and feed grinder, blacksmith shop, harness shop, brooder house, rabbit shed, washhouse, two woodsheds, and last but not least, the outhouse! About a quarter of a mile down the road, we had a sawmill where the boys worked cutting lumber. They also made pallets.

I never knew a dull moment at our home. We had so many animals to feed and take care of. We had horses, cows, pigs, chickens, and rabbits. We used the horses in the fields and to pull the buggies; the cows for milk; we sold the pigs; and we kept the chickens for both eggs and food.

I loved my little corner of the world, but I also realized early on that another world existed beyond the boundaries of our farm, and I looked forward to going to school. But, before I could start, I needed a vaccination.

My older brothers made a big deal about it, telling me how much it hurt and that when they got their shots, they cried for hours. This frightened me! Mom made plans with our neighbors, Dan and Mattie Troyer, to take Bennie and me at the same time. Bennie and I were about the same age and best friends, so going together felt better. We took the big double buggy and drove to Mount Pleasant Mills where we entered the health department.

I looked at Bennie and saw tears forming in his eyes so I quickly said, "I'll go first and let you know."

I saw instant relief spread over his face, and he said, "Good."

I felt the heat then. I knew that I had to act brave, so with my chin up and my shoulders back, Mom and I walked into the little room with the nurse. The stick of the needle wasn't half as bad as I thought and ended before I knew what happened.

I walked out and smiled at Bennie. "Not so bad," I said to his smiling face.

Then he walked into the room with his Mom, and very soon we headed home with instructions not to scratch it even if it itched. The nurse told us to expect a scab and we should leave it alone and let it simply fall off by itself. Bennie didn't follow the rules and scratched his scab off. It got infected and he had to go back to the doctor.

With our vaccinations behind us, the first day of school finally came. I felt nervous but excited. Mom made my lunch. I had an apple butter sandwich on homemade bread, a jelly jar full of chocolate milk, and some oatmeal cookies. She packed this in a peanut butter bucket and I went off with my brothers. We walked about a half-mile on a little dirt road toward the school, and my heart skipped with anticipation.

I already knew the teacher. My cousin Rachel taught the whole school, so that put my mind at ease. But I had no idea how many other children I'd meet, or what it would be like to be away from my mother for a whole day. I just figured that big kids went to school, and I sure saw myself as a big kid.

That first day of school, Rachel called on me. She said, "Emmy, would you please come up here to stand by my desk? I'd like for you to recite the alphabet and count as far as you can."

I almost panicked. What if I forgot the alphabet? What if I forgot how to count? The tears welled up in my eyes.

With tentative steps, I walked to the front of the room and stood at the teacher's desk. "A," I said in a little voice.

Rachel nodded for me to continue.

"B, C, D."

The teacher smiled. My confidence level soared. I didn't forget a thing. I recited the alphabet perfectly and counted clear up to 100 without a hitch.

"Very good, Emmy," Rachel said with a bright smile.

I beamed back and took my seat. I figured this school thing would work out just fine.

CZCZCZ

I frequently stayed after and helped the teacher clean the schoolhouse. In return she helped me. We didn't wear shoes during the summer months and sometimes not until fall. When the frost hit, my toes got numb on the cold road and felt frozen when I got to school. On these occasions, the teacher allowed me to sit by the big potbellied stove and study until my feet thawed out.

I enjoyed school very much. I spoke only Swiss and Dutch at home, and had fun learning how to speak English and feeling as though I lived in a part of the world. My grade included three girls and three boys, me, my best friend and cousin Lovina, Virginia, Elton, Leon and Bennie. Virginia, Elton and Leon were Mennonites.

The six of us made up a good class. I think we kept our teacher very busy at times! When the first morning bell rang, we'd rush to our seats. Then we'd all stand together and say The Lord's Prayer. Then we either sang songs or the teacher read to us from a book. I always preferred the singing. I loved to sing, but I felt painfully shy and it took me a long time to get up the courage to lead the class in a song. When I finally got up the nerve, I thoroughly enjoyed it!

In the first period we had reading or health, then recess. During second period we studied arithmetic. Then came spelling, English, writing, geography, and German. We didn't get all of these done every day because there wasn't enough time, so we alternated some of the classes. We did have reading, arithmetic, spelling, and English every day. The teacher never gave us homework. We had to do our school work at school because when we returned home, we had so many chores to do there wasn't time to do school work.

C3C8C8

At age six, my one chore was filling the wood boxes, a big job for me. We had a huge box in the kitchen and an even bigger one in the living room. In a big house like ours, with two bedrooms downstairs and four upstairs, we used lots of wood to keep warm. I used an ax to chop the wood pieces too big to fit into the stove.

During the summer, I had a different schedule. We kept a garden with all the vegetables and a truck patch where we grew sweet corn, potatoes, squash, cucumbers, watermelons, and things that took up more space. We hoed all of the vegetables every day. Mom had high standards for her garden. When the vegetables ripened, we harvested them and canned them for the winter.

I remember one summer when Mom ran short on

canning jars and asked me to get old Doll, our trustworthy mare that Mom always drove in the buggy. Excitedly, I ran out to the pasture to get Doll.

I thought we'd head off to the store, but when I got her all hitched up and ready to go, Mom got in the buggy and said, "Oh no, Emmy. We'll go to the dump and find some jars."

Though disappointed, I still thought the dump better than staying home and working!

When we got to the dump Mom found a couple of sticks and told me to search around with the stick and find old mayonnaise jars. After about an hour, we'd collected a big bunch of jars. We put them all in the back of the buggy and took them home where we washed them again and again. After cleaning them, we filled them with fresh peaches and sealed them.

I guess we didn't have the money to buy new jars. I never really thought of us as poor, but I think so now, in retrospect. We never had store bought bread or any prepared food from the store. Mom bought flour, sugar, and oatmeal in hundred-pound bags. We also bought spices and things like that. When my sister Fanny started dating, she wanted to buy some Crisco to make flakier pie crusts. She begged and begged until Mom finally gave in and let her buy some.

Fanny, an excellent cook, made good pies. She took particular care with how things looked, too. On Saturdays when we cleaned house, we always had to wipe off the furniture with vinegar water. We didn't have furniture polish. I sped through this job and didn't get the chair rungs clean enough. Fanny, the inspector, made me do them over and over until I got them clean enough to suit her. I always thought her too fussy about things like that. She called me a Tomboy and I called her a sissy. She got to stay in the house and cook meals and do girl stuff while I went out and helped in the fields.

Chapter 2

Amish History and Rules

The Amish church has a long history. Believers live in much the same way as their forefathers did. Many times when I asked questions about things that I didn't understand, someone invariably answered, "Because our forefathers did it this way."

The church members held an annual meeting to review and modify church rules. We usually scheduled this service each fall. It amounted to a normal church service after which all the baptized members stayed, and the men took charge of reviewing and revising the rules for everyone. They allowed women as members, and they could vote when ordaining a minister, but they got no say in setting the rules. Men, and other women, expected women to sit quietly and listen only.

I remember one woman's funeral when the preacher said, "I have great hopes for Mattie's soul, for she was a patient woman and a woman of few words."

At that moment, I felt like all bets for my soul flew out the window. I found it difficult to remain quiet and not give voice to my opinions and thoughts. However, Amish churches adopted different rules. Each community took responsibility for reviewing and revising their own rules.

However, one rule remained constant from church to church. Members must remain modest and unworldly. In our small community of ten to twelve families, women wore dresses of plain brown, black, gray or blue, not bright colors of green, red, pink, or purple. Only young girls could wear light colors. Dresses extended to mid-calf, with a hem no wider than one-and-a-half inch. The rules allowed small pleats or gathers at the waist. Rule-makers thought this the most modest look. Rules proclaimed unfitted bodices and only hooks and eyes or snaps for closure, and no buttons because they were considered decorative. Most of the women used straight pins.

They wore aprons about the same length as the dress, preferably about one-half inch shorter, pleated or gathered, with an attached belt about two inches in width. Women also wore a cape over the dress that tucked under the apron in the front and came to a point in the center back at the waist. We could have all of these pieces of the same color, or we wore black or white aprons and capes with colored dresses. Younger girls wore dresses much the same with a long straight apron. Unmarried women wore black caps, and married women wore white.

The men wore pants made of either blue denim or heavy black material with shirts made of the same material as the dresses. However, the rules allowed men to have buttons on their clothes. I never knew why.

Other rules included things like no drinking, no smoking, and no using any tobacco products. I didn't understand this either, because my Dad smoked home-rolled cigarettes and chewed Red Man tobacco as long as I could remember. He ranked as an elder of the church, and two of my brothers served as ministers. They pretty much made the rules and also made exceptions for themselves. My brother Pete, a minister, also chewed tobacco. Not very many people knew about it because he kept it hidden in the barn.

Other forbidden things included electricity, running water, phones, cars, automatic washers, chain saws, power lawn mowers, bicycles, dolls with faces, cameras, musical instruments, playing cards, dancing. The list goes on and on.

We weren't allowed stuffed furniture, only homemade cushions on our rocking chairs, and no pictures on the walls. Dad sat in his rocking chair after each meal and smoked a cigarette. He didn't use an ashtray but flicked the ashes on the floor and we swept them up later. He also made wine every summer. I never saw him drink it but it disappeared and he made more every year.

Our home fit the plain requirement, but we had warmth. Mom took care of that. A very warm, loving, generous woman who enjoyed people, she took every opportunity to visit with people, not only with Amish folks, but with everyone. She always made room at the table for anyone who might come along.

We had six bedrooms, a huge living room and kitchen, a large basement and a small ground cellar. A dirt floor covered half of the basement and felt quite cool. Here we kept bushels and bushels of potatoes, apples, carrots and other vegetables. On the shelves all around the walls we kept our canned goods. The front part of the basement had a wood floor, several small windows and a door to the outside. Here we kept big crocks of lard, Dad's wine and some things that we didn't want the light to damage. When Mom made cheese, she set it on the shelves to cure.

As a young girl, until I reached age ten, I slept in Mom and Dad's bedroom. My brothers Ben and Seppy and I all slept together in a big bed until Mom felt Ben had gotten old enough to move to a bedroom upstairs.

Ben walked in his sleep, and Mom worried that he'd jump out the window. As he got older, the sleepwalking seemed to decrease. However, one night Mom heard him go outside and waited for him to return. He didn't come back so Mom went looking for him and found him sitting on a milking stool in the milking parlor sound asleep wearing his underwear and his Sunday hat!

Mom asked, "Ben, what are you doing?"

He said very simply, "I'm waiting for the cows to come in."

Very gently she helped him back to bed.

One night after I'd reached the age to sleep upstairs, I heard him making a noise in his room. I thought I heard the window open and went to check on him. I found him standing by the open window, and it scared me half to death. I helped him back to bed and closed the window. The next morning we found some of his things on the ground beneath his window where he'd apparently thrown them. Mom told me that I also walked and talked in my sleep and that sometimes she heard us having conversations together in our sleep!

I don't remember when Buop got drafted during the war in Vietnam, but I remember that he came home occasionally for visits. He filed as a conscientious objector and spent four years working in a state hospital in Hershey, Pennsylvania. I remember on one of his visits he arrived in the middle of the night. I heard Mom get up to let him in the house and I got up as well.

He talked quietly to Mom about some of his experiences in the world. I remember hearing him tell Mom that he felt like he had big black marks on his back. I didn't know what he meant by that and feared that maybe he'd gotten hurt in some way. Later, someone explained to me he meant that maybe his working out in the world did not look good to God. He dated Bennie's big sister Mary at the time, and they got married soon after he came home to stay.

At ten years old I had to help with other chores. Mostly I fed animals and milked the cows. Most days started with Mom waking us to do the chores. First we fed the horses and cows, then while the cows ate, we milked them. Sometimes in the winter I froze by the time I got to the barn. The animals warmed me up. I remember cuddling up under the cows and getting just as close as I could!

Dad fed and took care of the pigs and Mom took care of the chickens. While we did the chores, Mom, Lydia, and Fannie fixed breakfast. Mostly we had oatmeal and eggs or pancakes. Sometimes for a special treat on Sunday, we had coffee soup. Mom made it with pieces of bread, which she poured sweetened coffee over. It tasted wonderful!

After chores we all went to the living room for morning prayers, then to the kitchen for breakfast. After breakfast our day began. During the school year we hurried off to school. During the summer we worked around the farm.

In the fall, we all went tomato picking. We lived close to the Susquehanna River and picked in the tomato fields along the river bottoms. We got up really early on those mornings and drove down to the river and picked tomatoes all day long for the owner. On longer distances, too far to drive our horses, the owners sent a school bus to pick us up. I loved those rides. Mom always went with us and picked tomatoes all day long while Dad stayed home and tended to things on the farm. On those rides, Mom entertained everyone with her sweet voice. She sang and yodeled with most everyone joining in to help her.

One early morning while driving on the highway in the fog, a semi truck that came around the corner scared the horse. She jumped off the road and we all landed in the ditch. I flew off the back of the buggy and went head first into the ditch, hitting my head on a rock. The horse and buggy turned upside down in the field. No one broke any bones and the horse seemed okay. We got everything turned right side up and went on to the tomato field. I had a terrible headache for several days.

We stayed busy all the time. We picked fruit in the orchards around us, or whatever grew in the season. We ate big lunches when we worked at home. Dad and all the boys came in at exactly noon. Mom made big meals with meat, potatoes, vegetables, and dessert. Maybe we ate only canned fruit for dessert, but we always had something. After the meal we washed the dishes, then did more chores.

In the winter it turned dark right after supper and on those evenings we had time to read books or write letters to our friends. I enjoyed reading *Uncle Tom's Cabin*, Laura Ingalls Wilder's *Little House on the Prairie*, *The Black*

Stallion, and *The Golden Stallion*. Because of our limited library, I read each book many times. Sometimes we played checkers. The boys got very good and usually beat me.

During the summer Mom grew all different kinds of tea. We picked it when she proclaimed it ready to harvest. We dried it on sheets out in the sun. Then she mixed it all together and we enjoyed a hot cup of tea every evening during the cold winter months.

At eight o'clock every evening, everyone gathered in the living room. One of us read a chapter from the Bible, then we all got on our knees and Dad said a prayer, the same long German prayer that I could never understand. Sometimes I fell asleep during the prayer! After that we all went to bed.

Grandma and Grandpa, Lydia and Mose Troyer, lived in the little house with their son August (Gust), born mentally challenged. Grandma got pregnant with him during the 1918 flu epidemic. They gave her medicine to keep her alive, but it caused damage to the baby. August could never talk but just made strange noises all the time. He frequently had *grand mal* seizures. They scared us kids because he made a horrible noise at the beginning then he fell out of the chair or bed.

I wasn't afraid of him otherwise because I saw him every day but he frightened some kids in the church. I guess he looked pretty scary. During the day he sat in a rocking chair rocking back and forth, playing with his toys. He liked best to play with post cards sewn together at one end. His tongue looked huge, and he always had his mouth open with his tongue hanging out. He wore a diaper all his life. Grandma trained him somewhat by putting him on a toileting schedule. Normally, when she put him on the toilet, he stayed until she came back to get him. Sometimes he didn't stay and I remember several times we saw him walking down the road stark naked! What a sight!

Grandma, a plump woman of five feet, seemed to stay in a pretty good mood most of the time. Sometimes though, I can remember her really getting aggravated at Grandpa, a very tall and slender man. He smoked a pipe and told great stories. When we had company he entertained us for hours. Everyone loved Grandpa.

As they grew older and needed help getting around, Mom fixed a bell on a rope so they could let us know when they needed us. She attached the rope to a big cowbell in our house. If they pulled on the rope, one of us went down to help them.

In April of 1966 Grandpa died of a massive heart attack. Mom, Dad, and my brothers were busy painting the barn as Grandma came running out of the house shouting.

"Help! Help! Help me please. It's Grandpa!" she yelled as she approached the barn.

Everyone dropped what they were doing and ran with her back to the house. By the time they got there, he had already died. He went quickly. I followed everyone and saw Grandpa lying there, dead. I gasped with shock, for I had never seen a dead body.

One of the boys went to town and called the undertaker who arrived in a big black hearse about an hour later. He looked very tall and wore a black hat and a long black coat. He had a little cot that he rolled down to the house, and in a little while he came back up with Grandpa on the cot. I couldn't see my grandfather because a blanket covered him.

The next morning, Mom and Dad took all the furniture out of their bedroom and placed a coffin in the corner. Dad and the boys made the coffin of pine boards the afternoon that Grandpa died. Mom placed a sheet inside and a small pillow. When they brought Grandpa back, the guys lifted him by his shoulders and feet and he stayed stiff as a board. This stiffness amazed me. The death experience frightened me a lot.

Grandpa lay very still in the coffin in the corner of the bedroom, and they put an oil lamp on top of the coffin so people could see his face. The lamp wasn't very bright and cast shadows on his face. I feared he'd suddenly wake up and begin to scream.

I woke several times during the night and each time heard noises downstairs. I wondered why, and finally got up the nerve to check it out. I found out when someone died, we had a wake, which means that someone stayed up all night, mostly the young folks. While they stayed awake with the body through the night, they baked pies, cookies, and cakes to feed people who came to visit and view the body.

Finally, after three days of having Grandpa in the bedroom, we held the funeral. They scheduled it like that to let people from other communities drive in. We held the service at our house, then the preacher nailed the top on the coffin and the boys carried it out and placed it in the back of our big double buggy.

They took Grandpa's coffin about a half mile down the road to the little cemetery at the corner of the little dirt road, and buried him there. Most of the people walked from our house. It rained a little that day and I looked down in the big hole the boys dug and saw a pretty big puddle of water. It bothered me a great deal that they put Grandpa down in that puddle of water.

After shoveling the last of the dirt, they put a piece of board at the head of his grave. It showed his name, birthday, and the day he died. I felt very sad that day.

Not long after Grandpa died, Grandma had a stroke and spent several weeks in the hospital. We didn't know if she'd make it or not, then suddenly she began to get better and soon came home. After that she and Gust lived with us in the big house where Mom could take care of them.

After the stroke, Grandma changed. She forgot everything and kept asking the same questions over and over again. Mom patiently answered her. She almost blew up sometimes, but before that happened she'd quietly walk out of the room.

Once when Mom left for a while I went looking for her. I found her in the attic, kneeling by an old milk can and praying. I left without disturbing her and went back to entertain Grandma. I got her interested in a book so when Mom came back she didn't start back in asking questions.

Grandma most often asked, "Where are all of my children?"

By the time we answered, she forgot and asked the same question again. Sometimes we all got very frustrated. Mom had nine brothers and sisters but they didn't ever offer to help her with Grandma and Gust.

One day Mom decided that Grandma needed a dog. She found an ad in the back of a magazine that advertised Rat Terrier puppies. She ordered two, a girl and boy. When they arrived, she named the female Topsy and the male Tip. Topsy had black-and-white spots and mostly white fur covered Tip, with a black spot on his face and on his left side. Grandma enjoyed having the cute little dogs on her lap.

One day a car, driven by a man named Gene, ran over Topsy, killing her instantly. After that day we always called him Topsy Killer. Tip seemed a little sad for a while, but he made friends with Cassy and loved running outdoors with her. Cassy gave birth to a litter of Tip's puppies. All tiny, some looked like Cassy and some looked like Tip.

We decided to keep a medium-sized male puppy with medium-long fur, a long flowing tail, and a small pointed face. He looked like a red fox. We named him Junior. Mom found another dog for Grandma, a tiny Toy Manchester which she name, Lucy Baines, after Lucy Baines Johnson, the president's daughter. Lucy turned out to be a great dog for Grandma. She loved nothing better than to sit in Grandma's lap. They formed a strong bond as buddies.

Life went on; births, deaths, marriages, and just plain living, and all according to church rules.

Chapter 3

John Flies In

When I was about twelve, we got a letter from John saying he'd planned a trip home. The letter said he'd taken flying lessons so to expect him in a small plane. He'd fly in from the southwest, fly over the hill, then circle the farm to let us know he'd arrived. After a couple circles he'd fly on to Selinsgrove to park the plane and rent a car. He said he'd arrive early Saturday afternoon.

His visit excited me, and so did the prospect of seeing the plane. I admired his mastery of flying, but when I expressed my excitement and amazement, Mom reprimanded me.

She said, "Don't get yourself all excited about such things. It's all part of the devil's work. Instead, you should pray that he stops flying, repents, and comes back to the church."

I only nodded demurely and walked away, secretly smiling. In my heart, I felt so very proud of John, and kept my excitement to myself.

That Saturday I asked to mow the lawn so I'd see John fly in. We had a large lawn and that summer got a push lawn mower. It didn't have a motor but I liked it better than cutting the grass with a blade. In the warm weather, I felt very hot and tired after mowing the entire yard. I went into the springhouse and sat on the cool concrete for about ten minutes. I splashed some cool water on my face then came out and sat in the back yard, watching for John.

Finally, I got up and went inside to sit on the couch by the window facing east. I sat there only a few moments when suddenly I heard a noise, looked out the window and saw, almost even with the window, a small plane.

I jumped up and ran out, shouting, "John's here!"

I ran into the back yard and jumped up and down waving my arms so he could see me.

Immediately my brothers and Dad surrounded me and said, "Stop it, Emmy."

With a puzzled look I asked, "Why?"

"What he's doing is evil. Stop encouraging him."

My heart sank. I just couldn't understand how anything as marvelous as flight could be evil. So I kept my thoughts to myself.

John and his friend Larry finally arrived a little later in a car. They visited for a couple of days and I had a wonderful time with him.

When the time came for him to leave, Dad cornered him. "John, you know you will most certainly go to hell if you refuse to repent and return home to the church."

"Dad, I just can't do it. This life isn't the right life for me."

"It's a Godly life. It's the right life!" Dad insisted.

"No, it's the right life for you. Not me."

Then Dad, with his face inches from John's, pointed

his finger into his son's chest and yelled at him. "Then you're going to hell!"

Seeing all this, I cried to Mom, "Please do something. Make them stop!"

My mother looked at me with a stern expression on her face. "You're father's right, and if you support John, you'll face the same fate."

God help me! I did support John. The realization hit me like a ton of bricks. I was going to go to hell! I ran into the house, got into bed, and cried and cried. My heart refused to accept what my parents said about John. His refusal to accept the Amish teachings didn't make him a bad person. On that day I realized that someday I'd leave the church as well, because I didn't believe what they preached.

We didn't have an ordained preacher at this time so church elders decided that we'd ordain one. Ordaining a preacher involved a whole day in church. The church allowed only married men as candidates, no matter their age. Following a regular church service, several of the elders went into a room and all the members of the church filed by the door and whispered their choice for preacher. The elders wrote down all the votes, then counted each.

The elders summoned the three men who received the most votes to sit at a table. In the middle of the table they placed three songbooks. One of the songbooks had a paper in it. They each had to choose a book and the man who chose the book with the paper in it got ordained. My brother Buop chose the book with the paper in it. He just bowed his head and cried, as did the rest of us.

In being ordained, he assumed an awesome

responsibility and took it very seriously. If anyone could do it, we all knew that Buop could. Some years later, elders ordained the tall, handsome Buop a bishop. I remember his round face, and warm eyes that expressed his love and kindness.

As the families in our small community grew, they all found the land more and more difficult to buy. Pete, Buop, and Lydia had married and lived in their own homes, all within three or four miles from us. Amish people didn't believe in birth control, so when young people got married, they had a baby, usually within a year. Mom wanted them to go to the hospital for the first one, then she helped them for the next ones. Pete came once in the middle of the night to get Mom. She had a bag packed and ready so she had only to dress and grab her bag. They got in the buggy and off they went. The next day she came home and announced a new baby in the family.

As I grew older, probably about fourteen, Mom sent me to care for the family while the mother healed. Mom always advised the mothers to stay off of their feet for six weeks after having a baby. She said it helped the uterus go back in place. When Lydia had her first baby I went to help her. Mostly I cooked meals for her husband Harry, cleaned house, helped with milking the cows, and helped take care of little Abraham whom we called Abie.

He was the cutest little baby, but he cried a lot. Lydia said he had colic. Many nights I walked and walked with him in my arms, bouncing and singing to him all the while. Finally, he'd fall asleep but not for long. He always woke up hungry. After he ate, he had more colic! Seemed like a vicious cycle to me. After a couple of weeks he got better.

All of Lydia's babies had colic.

Mary, Buop's wife, suffered a miscarriage in the sixth month of her pregnancy. They'd painted her kitchen, and the smell of the paint didn't agree with her. They rushed her to the hospital but couldn't save the baby boy. They named him John and buried him in the graveyard near Grandpa. He looked liked a tiny China doll, and lay in a casket so small that one person carried it. I thought him beautiful.

We buried John while three feet of snow covered the ground. A visiting preacher took care of the service in their home that day, and Buop sat with Mary, the twin to Lydia's husband Harry. I remember watching them and thinking how sad they looked. Mary, tiny and pale, looked like she would pass out at any moment. She wasn't strong enough to go to the gravesite and stayed at the house and rested.

Young people faced growing difficulties buying farms within our small community. Dad and the boys went in search of open land to start a new settlement. They found lots of available land in upstate New York that needed tilling. When they returned, Dad announced that we'd move. He didn't talk with Mom or ask her opinion, or anyone else's. He just made the announcement. Case closed. We'd move to New York whether we wanted to or not.

I'd turned fifteen and had finished school and began to substitute for the teacher when she needed help. I also helped with some of the young kids at school because I enjoyed it. Mom excused me from work at home on those days. She felt proud of me for helping out at school and always bragged on my intelligence to other people.

I looked forward to turning sixteen, the dating age, and I knew exactly who I wanted to date, Amos, the most handsome boy that God ever created. He lived nearby and I knew him as Ben's best friend. Growing up we spent a lot of time together and I felt sure that he knew, as well as I, that fate put us together. After all, Buop married his sister, Mary, and Lydia married his brother, Harry. I felt we'd marry someday. So the announcement that we'd move to New York upset me.

I talked to cousin Viny and she assured me that Danny Troyer and his family planned to move as well. Danny and Mattie Troyer had fourteen children. They lived near us next to the schoolhouse. Danny, a nephew of my Grandma's told great stories. Everyone loved him.

Dad and the boys planned an auction. We had to give up some of our belongings. Things that we'd had as long as I can remember, he planned to sell at auction to a stranger. I almost couldn't bear to think about it.

Mom seemed very sad these days because she did not want to leave the home we had known for so long. With her warm smile and kind words, she'd do anything for anyone in need, no matter who. I'd never seen my petite, dark-haired mother looking this unhappy, and it concerned me.

Dad and Mom never fought that I knew of but I wondered about this. She'd frequently go to her favorite spot in the attic now and pray about things that troubled her. The times that I found her there, she had tears in her eyes and looked so sad. It just tore at my heart.

A couple of weeks before the auction, a very pregnant Lydia asked me if I could come over to help her with chores because Harry had gone somewhere. Happy to help,

I went right over. As I drove up the road I saw another buggy behind me and it turned into the driveway.

Amos! He'd also come to help with the chores. We had about a dozen cows to feed and milk and some horses to take care of. So without talking much, we got through the chores okay. I felt a little disappointed at our lack of chances to talk, but while both of us worked in the milkhouse, he talked to me about our move.

"I'll really miss your family when you move, Emmy."

He didn't say anything about me in particular but I knew he meant that because it would have been too forward of him to do otherwise.

I felt myself blush at his words and just kept on milking the cow. The fates could yet conspire to keep us together.

On a sunny day in April of 1974, we had the auction. The auctioneer came early and we had lots of help getting the furniture in the front yard. The boys had gathered all the things from the barn and the outbuildings that they wanted to sell and filled the entire yard.

I looked through all the drawers from the cupboards to make sure we'd emptied them, and suddenly I had a great idea! Mom had bought me a pair of good, but very ugly shoes. I hated them and saw this as my way to get rid of them.

I found a brown paper bag and wrapped those shoes up, found a big drawer and hid them way in the back. I watched and waited until that cupboard sold and moved out. I took an easy breath when I saw it lumbering down the drive in the back of someone's truck! I felt very lucky that I didn't get caught, but at least nobody could make me wear them again!

I watched Mom as she walked through the aisles of furniture. She stopped from time to time and very lovingly ran her hand over the top of a dresser that the family had owned for years and years. I wanted to change all this for her and take away the hurt, but I couldn't.

As the auctioneer sang his song, our furniture disappeared piece by piece, and soon the crowd moved on out to the barn. I sat on a bench that the new owner hadn't picked up yet when Seppy came running breathlessly from the blacksmith shop.

"Emmy, come quick. They're gonna sell the farm!"

I wanted to tell him not to get so excited, but I didn't. I just swallowed hard and slowly walked to the shop where a small group of people huddled together as the auctioneer talked about our farm. He didn't know anything about it. We knew every inch of it.

We built huts in the woods and knew all the trails. I could find every place I went hunting; knew where the raccoons had their babies; where to find the biggest woodchuck hole; where we picked blackberries and cherries; and where you could drink the water that came up through the ground. I knew where you could catch the most fish; where the best swimming hole was; and where the snakes hung out.

As the bidding began, I looked around. I couldn't tell who bid, but soon I saw Danny Troyer nod his head every time the auctioneer looked that way. I looked over at Amos and he just stood there looking at his feet. Ben stood beside him so I walked over. He looked up and smiled at me. Ben and Amos, the best friends, looked sad about leaving each other. Finally, after what seemed like forever, the bidding ended and Danny Troyer owned our farm. In a way I felt glad that he bought it. Good friends of our family, they'd take care of the place. But this also meant they wouldn't move to New York. My fear of leaving Amos in Pennsylvania was coming true.

Chapter 4

New York Farms

The family purchased two farms in Norfolk, New York, for Pete and Buop and their families. They'd move first, then look for a farm for Mom and Dad. Mom asked me to move with Pete and his family because Pete and Susan expected a baby at the end of the month. They already had four children, Christy, Roman, Susie, and Margaret, but they weren't old enough to help with the new baby.

Knowing that I didn't have a choice in the matter, I agreed to go. I'd never traveled away from home before and didn't look forward to this, especially so far away from Mom. The thought of a totally strange place where the locals weren't used to seeing Amish people frightened me. On April 11, 1974, Pete, Christy, and I got in the U-Haul truck and started our trip to this unknown place. Pete's English friend drove the truck for us. Susan and the rest of the family traveled in a van, also driven by an English friend.

It took us two days to get to Norfolk. As we got closer I felt a strong dislike for the place. Everything looked cold and bleak. No green grass, all appeared frozen and brown. I saw no leaves on the trees, not even buds. I could see long and hard winters in our future. To top it all off, it had rained and mud covered everything. We finally arrived at Pete's place and the real shocker hit me! The house, a ramshackle structure, smelled like dirty cats and dogs, and the smell had penetrated the rotting walls and floors. As I began to climb the stairway to the second floor, the stairs broke away beneath me. My nightmare had begun!

Somehow we made it through those days. Susan kept a good attitude, even though pregnant. We tried to break ground beside the house to start a garden. We found the sod thick and heavy, difficult to break up, and the roots hard to get rid of. Slowly we got it worked up and by the time we could plant, we had a nice spot ready.

Pete and Buop looked for a farm for Mom and Dad. One day Pete came home and asked me if I'd like to see where we'd live. He took me to Brookdale, a small village, and turned left into a long driveway with huge maples on each side. The beautiful farm included a six-bedroom red brick house and a big red barn. The garden sat across the driveway from the house and a small creek ran down below. The beautiful new home gave me hope.

On April 30, Susan gave birth to a daughter they named Rhoda. My sister Lydia, who still lived in Pennsylvania, had a baby girl the same day and named her Mattie. I thought of my brother Ben, also born on this day. Susan went to the hospital to have the baby since Mom wasn't there to help her deliver. I took care of the other kids and chores around the house while she recovered. Pete got a sawmill set up so he could begin to cut lumber for a new house. He planned to have it ready by fall for the family.

Buop and his family moved into a place about a mile down the road. The people who lived there scheduled an auction in preparation for their move. We went over and all the English people stared at us. One little girl walked up to me and touched me.

With big eyes, she looked amazed and said, "Look, Mommy, she's real."

I felt like an animal in a zoo. I just wanted to disappear.

In May, Mom, Dad and the rest of the family moved up. I'd felt so lonely, and then so happy to see them! Mom seemed happy with our new home. Franie liked it as well. The boys went right to work taking out the wall to the small kitchen, making it much larger. They took out all the electric lights and the electric well pump. Then they put two hand pumps next to the sink. One went to the well and the other went to the cistern, which had rainwater in it. We used that to do laundry and other cleaning because of the soft water. We used a huge wood furnace in the basement to heat the major portion of the house. The ductwork went to the first floor, then we had open registers to the upstairs.

That month I turned sixteen and had no one to date because the only young Amish folks around were part of our family. Soon, people came for visits. The young folks consisted of single people sixteen and older. Usually they all met after church at the home where we had church. They all ate supper together and after washing the dishes, sat around the table, talked, and sang songs. We sang in German using different songbooks than those from church.

The singing style differed, too. In church we had a certain singing style that sounded almost like chanting, very slow, and each word took forever, or so I thought!

After the singing, the boys could ask a girl if he could drive her home. If she said yes, he drove her to her home and they'd go inside and she served a dessert and a beverage. He'd stay for awhile, then go home. However, all the boys were either my brothers or cousins! I still felt an infatuation for Amos and waited for the day he'd arrive for a visit.

I didn't have much time to think about it, though, as we cleared off land to till. We dug out huge rocks. The boys built a platform that the horses could pull across the ground. When we got the rock dug out they put a chain around it and pulled it up on the platform with the horse, then hooked the horse to the platform and dragged it off.

Clearing the land made for hard work, and cutting the trees down with the old crosscut saw took forever. One Sunday the boys and Dad decided they could use a chain saw. I wondered how they could arbitrarily decide when things were no longer "of the devil."

When I asked Mom about that, she said, "It's not up to you to question the leaders of the church."

That didn't sound right to me, but I decided not to pursue it any further.

That fall Pete finished a nice two-story home and moved his family in. Susan loved the clean new house and they decided to use the old house as a school. They took out a wall and put a wood stove in the center, put a bunch of desks in, and school started.

The next spring, more families moved in, which meant

more young folks. Dad and the boys needed an implement shed and granary so they took all the trees we cut down to Pete's sawmill to cut into lumber. Not long after, a school bus full of men from Pennsylvania came up and they built the entire thing in one day! Amos came with the group and I got so excited to see him! My cousin Neal came, too. I talked to him a little about Amos and he said I should talk with him. I never got up the nerve to say anything. They stayed for a couple of days. We had church and the young folks got together for a singing, but Amos never said anything to me.

Later that year, Amos's brother Joseph moved up with a couple of other young men. Soon I heard that he planned to ask me for a date. That sounded crazy. But then my cousin Viny informed me that Amos and our cousin Fanny were already dating on a steady basis. The news shocked me and my heart dropped.

I had always thought of Amos as mine and felt that someday we'd end up together. A couple months later, Joseph asked if he could take me home after a singing and I said he could. I thought him very nice and the boys and Mom and Dad liked him. They all thought we'd get married, but I knew that I'd never get married and strap myself down with a big family in this church for the rest of my life. I knew that wouldn't make me happy. I wanted a life that made sense to me.

Mom always allowed us to have English friends. She even let them come spend the summers with us on the farm. My two nieces, Patty and Pam, John's daughters, came to spend the summer with us in 1975. Mom let me get out of chores if I entertained them. We had so much fun!

We explored the entire 279 acres and found sand dunes where lots of turtles came and buried their eggs to let them hatch. We played in the sand taking care not to hurt the turtle eggs. We buried each other in the sand up to our necks. Patty brought a camera, off-limits to me on either end of it. After I buried them both in the sand, they talked me into taking their picture. No one saw us and I didn't think I'd get found out. Later Mom discovered the picture and she knew only I could've taken it. This put me in a ton of trouble.

I didn't talk to Patty and Pam about wanting to leave home because I feared they'd tell someone. So I talked to my friend Jody, an English friend that I got to know through one of my brothers. She said if I needed help, she'd help me. Overwhelmed, I couldn't think about it for too long. I had no idea how to get away and feared thinking about it very seriously.

That fall as Mom and I butchered chickens, I mentioned my thoughts to her. "Mom, I really need to talk to you. I've been thinking about leaving the church."

"Stop. Stop right there. Don't give in to the temptations of the devil. Don't even have the tiniest thoughts about anything of the sort."

"But, Mom."

"Stop! If you continue with these thoughts, you'll surely burn in hell forever."

I didn't bring it up again. Soon after that Mom and my brothers Pete, a minister, and Buop, a bishop, encouraged me to join the church. I didn't feel the urge but Mom wanted me to so I joined the other young folks and we made our vows to God and joined the Old Order Amish

Church in the summer or 1976, the Bicentennial year, and I felt quite content for the time.

I still dated Joseph and kept very busy on the farm. Some of my brothers worked in Pete's sawmill and as carpenters elsewhere. Mom, Franie, and I baked and made cottage cheese and butter to sell. Mom had laying hens which kept us busy selling eggs as well. We baked on Thursdays, and Mom woke us up very early to get the dough started. She made bread, Franie made cinnamon rolls, and I made doughnuts.

Most days I made about a hundred dozen doughnuts. We made everything on the wood stove, even during the summer. I had a huge canner full of pork grease that I fried the doughnuts in. Sometimes I felt my skin might boil off of my face as I stood over the hot stove turning those doughnuts. The grease smell made me sick. I wished for the outdoors, working in the fields.

In July, as I drove through Norfolk in my buggy with my old mare, Tisma Wick, I could see that the road had closed in town and saw lots of people standing around. Since I couldn't get through, I tied the horse up and went to check it out. What I saw amazed me. I saw big, beautiful floats and people marching! They called it a parade!

I stayed and watched until it ended, then went home. I couldn't wait to share this with everyone at home. I quickly saw my mistake.

The next Sunday as church ended, Pete stood up and announced to the entire church that all members should stay seated.

After all the children and non-members left, he announced, "One among us had sinned and needs to make it right with God and the church." His eyes bore into me.

I had seen a parade! I hadn't sinned! Where was the sin?

"You know who you are." His voice boomed through the church.

I stood on shaky legs and made my way to the front of the church, and lied.

"Yes, I've sinned. I watched a parade in town. But I promise never to do such a thing again. I beg forgiveness of God and of all of you."

I felt the heat rise in my face. Utter embarrassment suffused me. I felt confused and angry and once again seriously considered leaving the church. I felt the unfairness of confessing something I didn't believe wrong.

Back at home, I said to Mom, "I still don't feel I did anything wrong. Pete was wrong for making me stand up there and ask for forgiveness."

"You did wrong. You had to confess and ask forgiveness. Pete was right to do what he did. That's all there is to it," she said steadfastly.

I could see that she'd never change how she felt, no matter what I said, so I just walked away.

I had been raised in the church, in this life, but I felt like an outsider. I resented it, and my brother Pete. I knew I could never be happy here. A new question stirred in my mind then: Could I find the strength to leave?

CBCBCB

That winter Mom delivered a baby girl for Laura and Amos Eicher, their thirteenth child. They lived on a farm about three miles from our house. When they brought Mom home she told me to pack a bag and go home with them to help out.

I went upstairs, threw a couple of things in a bag, feeling like screaming, but all the while kept a smile on my face, got in the buggy and went home with them. That clinched it for me. I had to cook, clean house, do laundry, and help with outside chores. Cooking wasn't so bad, but I had to cook in great quantities. Cleaning wasn't so terrible because the older children helped me. But three children in diapers made for a lot of laundry. I felt like I did laundry all the time. Without disposable diapers, I heated water and poured it into a big tub with a handle that I had to move back and forth to create a stirring motion. This rubbed the clothes together to get them clean. Then I ran them through the wringer and hung them out to dry.

My fingers grew numb in the cold, and occasionally wet fingers stuck to the clothesline. I quickly put some wet clothes over my hand to unhook it from the frozen line. To me, doing everything the hard way made no sense. After six weeks of that, I felt great joy in going home!

That winter something happened to our schoolteacher and she wasn't able to finish the year out. The elders asked me to teach as I had some experience with this. They'd pay me three dollars a day. Mom and Dad got the money so the pay didn't matter to me. I agreed and loved teaching those bright children, most of them my nieces and nephews.

Many of them had bad grades at this point, and I wanted to help them do better so I made a deal with them. I started a paper chain and hung it up on the wall then told all the students that for each "A," they'd get to make a paper loop in the color of their choice and hang it up. When the chain reached all the way around the room we'd have a party with no class for an entire day, just good food and games all day.

They got so excited and performed very well. Every day we put new loops up on the wall and the room looked so festive with all the different colors. We had about ten feet left to go when one of the elders came to visit the school one afternoon while the children were leaving.

"Hello, Emmy," the elder said as he walked in the door.

"Good afternoon, Elder. How are you today?"

He looked around the room and said simply, "You must take the chain down."

I gave him a puzzled look and asked, "Why? The children love it and it helps them do so much better in their studies."

"It's too fancy. You must take it down." Without another word, he took his leave.

I hated that so much. I fought back the tears as I tore down that paper chain, but the children and I had a party day anyway.

While teaching school I stayed with Pete and his family, who lived just across the street. While living with them, I met a friend of Pete's named Carl, who lived just down the road with an older man we called Uncle Rob. Carl and Uncle Rob hauled lumber and did other things for Pete. I thought Carl very handsome, and he spoke to me whenever he visited. A couple times when I walked to or from our house to Pete's house, Carl and Uncle Rob gave me a ride.

That summer I turned nineteen. I'd just finished with the school year and knew that the time had come to break from my family and the church. One of the girls, Lizzie Peachy, and I housesat for some English people and I had access to the telephone. I talked to my brother John a couple of times and spoke with him about my desire to leave the church. He didn't encourage me and he didn't offer to help as I'd hoped. I guess he knew the difficulties and didn't want to see his little sister go through all that. Even though I thought of myself as a big girl, capable of anything I set my mind to, he knew things about this huge change that I didn't.

I came up with a simple plan to take a little money from the family stash for living on for a short time. I didn't feel bad about this because with all the baking and teaching and working for families, all the money went to Mom and Dad. I didn't have any money of my own. After I managed to make the break from the family, I'd go to Indiana where I'd stay with my nieces, Patty and Pam, get a job, and go from there. I thought the rest would be smooth sailing.

I spoke with Jody about my plan and she still wanted to help me. Jody and Uncle Rob's nephew, Harry, planned to marry. I spoke about my plans with Carl and Uncle Rob as well, and they also offered to help me. I began to feel good about it, excited even. Jody and I came up with a day and when I next saw Joseph, I broke up with him. Upset, he left very quickly.

On June 26, everyone went to church at Buop's house. We took turns staying home with Gust, and that day I stayed. Jody planned to come pick me up about fifteen minutes before Mom and Dad arrived home. I didn't want to leave Gust alone for long. By now Grandma suffered from severe dementia and couldn't take care of Gust. She went to church with Mom and Dad.

I packed a few of my things and took sixty dollars to buy a bus ticket to Indiana. Then I waited for Jody.

I couldn't decide what kind of note to leave for Mom. I didn't want to just disappear, because I didn't want them to worry, and yet she'd feel devastated if she thought I'd left the church. So I made a very bad decision and let Jody write a note saying she'd come to get me and not to worry. If I could do anything over, I'd have written the note for Mom because when she read Jody's note, she thought something terrible had happened to me.

Jody took me to her sister's house and stayed with me the first night. We planned to get some English clothes the next day and look into getting a bus ticket.

Late that evening, Pete knocked on Carl's door and talked with him, telling him that Mom felt very ill and needed to know that I was okay. Carl told him where I'd gone because he knew of my close relationship with my mother and that I loved her very much. Pete promised they'd let me leave again if only I'd go home with him and let Mom see me with her own eyes. I told Pete that since he promised, I'd leave with him.

I got in the buggy and we headed for home. I felt uncertain about going back home, but I needed to see Mom myself, and let her see me. I didn't want her to be sick and worried about me.

As we drove toward the house, Pete asked, "Emmy, why do you want to leave?"

I only hoped my words could make him see my point

of view. "Pete, I don't feel the Amish way is the right way for me. I don't agree with the rules and the control they have over the people in the church."

"Emmy, you don't mean that. You only left because you need a man."

Suddenly the door flew open and Mom and Dad and the whole family came running out. The boys came to the buggy, picked me up and carried me into the house. Immediately, they locked the doors and closed the curtains. I knew then that Pete had lied when he said Mom seemed almost ready to die. She seemed fine. They'd tricked me, and I knew they'd try to keep me from leaving again.

The family huddled together and prayed while my brother Chris went to get the bishop and his daughter Martha, my good friend. Soon they arrived and everyone continued to pray. They stopped for a while and asked me lots of questions about why I left. They wouldn't accept my answers. Finally at four in the morning I asked Mom if I could go to bed. She allowed me to go if Martha stayed with me.

During the night I had to use the toilet and went downstairs. When I got to the bottom of the stairs I ran into something. Mom had pulled the couch against the stairway and slept there so she'd know if I went downstairs.

"What do you want down here?" she asked.

Still bleary-eyed from sleep I answered, "I need to use the toilet."

"All right, then. Let's go." She walked me out to the toilet and waited for me, then walked me back upstairs.

The next morning, the family told me to stay in my room and wait for someone to bring breakfast to me. For the next three days they brought meals to me and walked with me to the toilet when I had to go, each time admonishing and questioning me.

I still felt so angry and disillusioned by everything that I refused to cooperate. I kept thinking about how to escape. I thought about tying sheets and blankets together and climbing out the window, but Mom and Dad slept in the bedroom directly beneath mine.

After the third day, I heard a noise and looked out my window. I saw a van with blue license plates enter the driveway. Soon after that I saw lots of buggies come in. I knew this meant something important in the offing. Curious to discover what, I eavesdropped at the register but couldn't hear a thing. Mom had the door to her bedroom closed and no one came up to talk with me.

Suddenly, I heard a noise in the bedroom below me and as I listened at the register I could hear a couple of women speaking very quietly. One of them put a baby down for a nap. I couldn't hear their words. When they left the room, the door stayed ajar and I could very faintly hear voices. I continued to listen and then I could hear someone say my name and finally put it all together.

The van had come from Pennsylvania. My sister Lydia came up in it and they made plans for me to go home with her, where she'd keep me in her basement until I mended my evil ways. This shocked me to action. I knew I had to do something very quickly.

As I lay on my bed contemplating what I should do, I heard a knock on my door and Martha came in. I looked at her and began to cry.

"Martha, please tell everyone that I was confused. I

didn't know what to think. I don't really want to leave the church. I was just confused. Let's go downstairs and tell everyone."

"Are you sure, Emmy? Do you really want to stay?" Her eyes looked so bright with happiness.

"Yes, Martha. I want to stay." I hated lying to her, but I felt my very survival was at stake.

Martha took me downstairs, and Mom seemed so happy to see me. I felt guilty, because I knew just as soon as I could figure out a way, I'd leave again.

As I stood talking with Martha I wanted so badly to get on my horse and just ride away. Suddenly, I put a plan together. I'd ask Mom if Martha and I could go riding. I did just that, and she happily agreed and asked Chris to get my horse. A few moments later we left our driveway.

Still trying to put my plan together, I told Martha I wanted to stop at the neighbors and let them know I was okay. Martha agreed and held my horse for me while I went in to see them. I quickly asked them if I could make a phone call and called Jody. She wasn't home but I spoke to her fiancé, Harry.

I explained my situation and he said, "Fine, I'll pick you up along the road. I'll make up some story for Martha, I don't know what right now, but whatever it is, just go with it."

My heart fluttered at the prospect of freedom.

Martha and I continued on our ride. We turned down a little dirt road that had very little traffic. About halfway down that road I saw a Volkswagen Beetle approaching and prepared myself to escape.

Harry stopped the car near us and said, "Do either one

of you know how to help a woman have a baby?"

I felt shaky, but said, "I do. I can help you out." I climbed down off of my horse and turned to my friend. "Martha, I'm leaving. He came to take me out of here."

"Emmy, no, you can't do this."

With determination I said, "I can and I will. Good-bye, Martha."

She began to cry, turned her horse around and quickly rode away. I tied my horse in a safe place and got in the car. Harry tried to start the car but the engine wouldn't turn over. Since I didn't know how to drive a car, I had to get out and push until it finally started!

He took me to Jody's house. I felt happy to see her, and to escape, but now I had no idea how to get to Indiana because Mom made sure that I had no money.

Jody said, "We'll figure something out, Emmy."

She took me to her sister's summerhouse, on an island in the St. Lawrence Seaway. I cried most of that first night. I felt very bad for deceiving Mom again and very much alone out there. I got scared all alone in that house.

Jody came to see me every day, and one day she came with a message from Chris. He said he wanted to see me and asked if we could meet in a place of my choice. Jody and I talked about it. I wanted to see him but I feared that my family planned to lock me up again.

"You know, you could go if I drive you and Carl drove Chris," Jody suggested. "We could meet in a big parking lot and stay in our cars, just talk from the windows."

Chris agreed and we met. I felt very awkward because of all the teachings about submissiveness, and girls doing as told by the boys. Standing up to my older brother proved difficult. He asked questions about my plans, how I'd survive. He said I wasn't trained to live in the world and saw homelessness in my future.

He sure didn't paint a rosy picture.

Chapter 5

A Proposal of Marriage

Again, I cried all night. I feared going back and feared living on my own, and I didn't think I could support myself. The next day Carl came by. He said he wanted to get me off the island and take me for a little ride. I felt happy to go. He asked me about my plans, and of course I didn't have any. He asked me how I felt about getting married.

"Look, if we get married, your family has to leave you alone, plus you'd have a place to live."

I thought about it, realized that I'd get no better offer, and decided to accept. I felt an attraction to him although I really hadn't planned to get married, and I also knew that I didn't love him.

He took me to meet his family, his three sisters and parents. We quickly began to make plans for the wedding. His mom and dad treated me kindly and I loved his three sisters. I had to take care where I went and couldn't go anywhere by myself now because my family had found out where I stayed.

Mom made friends with the Indians from the

reservation and one tall man named Big Bear told Mom he had a vision and saw me in street clothes walking in town. So then the Indians started looking for me too. I didn't tell anyone about getting married because I knew they'd really try to stop me then.

One day I got word that Mom wanted to see me and that she'd come by herself to Uncle Rob's house. I met her there and we visited.

"Emmy, please tell me again why you wanted to leave. Wasn't life good with us? Weren't you happy?" she asked.

"Mom, we've been through all this before. I just don't see myself living the Amish way for the rest of my life. There's a whole world out there and I want, no, I need to be a part of it."

She didn't accept my explanation. "Emmy, are you with child?"

"No! I haven't done anything to cause a pregnancy."

She ignored my answer and leaned closer to me. "Just come home, Emmy. We'll all help out with the baby."

I folded my arms over my chest. "No, I'm not coming home."

She left crying.

The family knew that I went to Rob's house from time to time so they watched the house. Carl and I planned to get married there. His sister Kathy made my dress and she also helped me get some makeup. I found applying mascara difficult and at first I thought my eyes didn't look natural wearing it.

The day before the wedding I stayed at Jody's mother's house. The next day a little green dump truck pulled into the driveway and Carl and Harry came in. They carried a large barrel and told me that they planned to help me into the barrel, load the barrel onto the truck, drive to Rob's house, and carry the barrel into the house.

"Don't you see? This is perfect. No one will know you're in the house," Carl said.

I agreed and after I had safely arrived at the house, I dressed and we stood in front of the big fireplace and the justice of the peace married us. During the short ceremony I almost lost consciousness. I felt something pushing on my lungs, everything got very dark, and my knees began to buckle. I reached up and held on to the mantle, took a deep breath and in a few minutes I felt okay. Now married, I knew I couldn't back out. I'd certainly not planned this, but I told myself that perhaps the Lord made this plan for me.

Carl treated me well and seemed very happy having me around. We lived in Norfolk with Uncle Rob, a very pleasant man and a good cook. I didn't know men could cook like that. Every day I learned lots of new things. Carl took me to the drive-in movie and we saw *Grease*. I sat with my eyes glued to the screen and felt amazed at the big picture on the wall. I had no clue how it worked and didn't understand it when someone explained it to me.

Soon I started to learn how to drive the car, a fun but nerve-wracking experience. Sometimes Uncle Rob and Carl both sat in the car telling me what to do. What a mess! When I finally took my test and passed with flying colors, Carl gave me the car, a small green Ford Charger. I got so excited!

I still took care when going out for fear of getting kidnapped. On several occasions Ben and Chris hid outside the house waiting for me to come out. One morning soon after Carl left the house to go to work, I heard a knock on the door. I thought he had forgotten something but when I opened the door, there stood Chris.

"I'm not here to hurt you, Emmy, and I don't plan to take you home. I just want to talk to you."

I let him in. We had a nice talk and he apologized and said if he had any say in it, they wouldn't treat me this way.

"So why did you come over so early?"

"I hid up in the tree all night long, waiting for a time to come in to see you. I miss you, Emmy, and though I wish you'd come home, I know that's never going to happen."

He broke my heart, but I couldn't turn back now.

Another time I woke up during the night and heard whispering outside my open window. That night we found Ben and Chris hiding in the bushes.

Then Ben confessed. "We were waiting for you to come outside so we could knock you out and take you home."

They just never gave up.

A little over a month after Carl and I married, I felt very sick and wanted to throw up all the time. I felt worse in the mornings.

Carl took me to see Dr. Dobies who said, "Emmy, you're going to have a baby."

I cried for a week because I didn't feel like I wanted a baby. Carl promised me that we wouldn't have a lot of kids. That made me feel better and I soon cheered up.

That fall Carl started his own business. He made wood shingles out of cedar. He worked in an old garage and when I felt up to it, I'd go out and help him. Some days I still felt very nauseated and other days I felt better. However, I continued to lose weight instead of gaining.

In October, I went to see Dr. Dobies again and he said, "Young lady, you've got to eat everything you can get your hands on, even eat the plate!"

I had to laugh at the picture that painted in my brain.

"I suggest you make a cheeseburger and a milk shake and eat it just before going to bed at night."

I did as he said and began to gain some weight back.

When I went to see the jovial Dr. Dobies again the next month, he told me I'd gained twelve pounds. "Okay, you're headed in the right direction. Now you can slow down a little on the eating."

Soon I felt much better and went to work in the shingle mill every day. The cedar wood smelled very nice and I felt happier than I had since I left home. I enjoyed fitting the shingles in a bunch and I could sing along with the radio all day long. I loved music and listened to it as often as I could. During the week we worked hard, and on weekends we went out to visit Carl's parents. Sometimes we went to Canada to visit his grandparents. We also spent time at a camp where some of his family had a summerhouse.

I had very little contact with my family. I called my brother John, who lived in Hanover, Indiana. We didn't know one another well and I didn't feel like he really wanted to get to know me. He never called me. I think he believed I'd eventually go back home and just didn't want to get involved.

I also contacted Viola, John's ex-wife, who grew up Amish. She lived in Madison, Indiana, only a few miles from Hanover. I knew her much better than I ever knew John because she came to live with us for a while after her divorce and she brought Patty and Pam to spend summers with us. She wanted Carl and me to come for a visit. I talked with Carl and he said he'd like for me to see them, so we decided to go at the first opportunity.

I missed my family very much and wanted to see them. Especially with the pregnancy, I wanted my mother. I cried after every visit or phone call. I felt they brainwashed me as a child and told me that only the Amish way was the right way and anything else led straight to the devil and hell. I knew better but when they bashed me over and over, I began to waiver in self-doubt. I knew I wasn't a bad person but they told me that just for living in the "world" my soul would most surely go straight to hell, where I'd beg for just one drop of water to cool my burning tongue. I'd surely burn for all eternity, they said.

Listening to that over and over tore me down emotionally. I often wondered if maybe I did act sinfully. I didn't want to go to hell. Sometimes I thought I should return home just in case. Question after question raced through my mind until I felt crazy.

I tried to think about all of the consequences. If I stayed away, I'd miss my family terribly, but I'd live in the way that I wanted to, with my own family. If I went back to them, I'd depend on them totally because of my pregnancy, and I could never marry because they didn't believe in divorce. I struggled and dreaded visits from them.

One day as we worked in the shingle mill, a blue van pulled in and a man got out and came to the door. Carl went to greet him. They talked for a few minutes, then came on in. I looked up in shock when I recognized an old acquaintance from Pennsylvania, Troy, who drove Amish people around in his van.

We talked for a few minutes then he asked me how I was.

"I'm fine, Troy. Thanks for asking."

He said, "You know, your brothers asked me to come. They wanted me to take you for a ride and deliver you to them. They offered me money, but I just couldn't do it."

We talked for a few more minutes then he left. For weeks after that I feared leaving the house alone.

Right before school started, I got a call from the woman who planned to teach. She asked me if I'd come by the schoolhouse and go over some of the books with her, as she had never taught school and didn't know what books went with what grades. I told her I'd love to help and we set a day and time to meet at the schoolhouse. The day arrived, and worry nagged at me. What if they tried to kidnap me again?

I tried to put it out of my mind but felt afraid and borrowed my neighbor's car to keep from being recognized and drove by the school to see if I saw anyone there. As I passed, it all looked very quiet but when I looked closer, I saw four buggies tied behind the schoolhouse. Nobody ever parked back there before so I felt certain of another trick. I turned around and returned home, feeling violated.

I talked with Viola often. She called on a regular basis to check on me and the pregnancy. She acted like a mother to me. I did, however, really want to get to know John better, and I think Carl knew that because one day about the first of November, as we talked about Christmas, he asked if I'd like to go see John for Christmas. I got so excited!

We borrowed a friend's camper pickup truck. We

cleaned it up and stocked it with food. I thought it so cute. At almost five months pregnant, I felt a little uncomfortable when I sat in one position too long. I also had to use the bathroom quite frequently.

We left with a camper full of supplies and an Atlas. I thought this a great adventure. As we got further down state we saw more snow. We took a weather detour off the interstate and had to drive through a part of Buffalo. The snowbanks beside the road stood taller than our truck. We finally got back on the interstate and moved along nicely when another vehicle lost control and ours got pushed onto the shoulder. The right wheel got caught in the snow and took us down into the median. I thought we'd turn over, but Carl kept it under control and somehow drove it right back up and onto the road without ever stopping.

We had no other mishaps on the trip. We stopped and took short walks every couple of hours. I felt very cold and always happy to get back into the truck. Driving through Pennsylvania and Ohio seemed to take forever. When we got close, we called John and he gave us directions to his house. We found it easily and seeing him made me so happy. I thought him very handsome and I felt so proud of him. He worked as a State Trooper for the State of Indiana. Their house appeared clean and neat with not a thing out of place, and I almost felt afraid of moving around or sitting down anywhere.

Gail, his wife, had short, curly blond hair, freckles, and a sweet smile. She made us feel welcome and talked with me about my pregnancy. It wasn't easy for me to talk about this since the Amish taught us not to talk about those things. Around home, everyone saw pregnant women but no one talked about it. Gail must have known how I felt because she began to share things with me about her pregnancies. John and Gail had two children, John Jr. and Lisa. I enjoyed our visit so much.

The next day we went to see Viola and her family. She married Charlie, who had two daughters, so now they had Patti, Pam, Linda, and Beverly. I felt close to Viola and enjoyed my visit with her. We talked about the way my plans changed after I left home and how I wanted to come to Indiana but the second time I left I didn't have any money and felt pretty much stranded. She asked me if I'd like to stay with them. I appreciated the invitation and wanted to stay but didn't think it right to leave Carl, so I declined. Pam turned fourteen in the spring, and Viola said she'd send her to help me with the baby after school let out. I felt better because I had no idea how I'd manage without help.

I don't remember much about the rest of the winter, except that the cold kept me indoors most of the time watching soap operas during the day. I liked *The Young and the Restless* the best. I took classes to get my GED in a motor home that came to town and parked in the courthouse parking lot. I went one day a week until I completed it and received my certificate. I enjoyed it, and felt proud of myself.

The rest of the winter just kind of slipped away. As the months went on, I found it harder to get around and felt some very lonely times. Some days I sat around and cried for hours. I missed my family very much and I felt alone all the time.

One day, one of my brothers called to say that

Grandmother had gone to the hospital and while she was responsive, she didn't recognize them. I got dressed and immediately went to the hospital to see her. My uncle Dan sat with Grandma when I arrived. When he saw me he immediately came to greet me. Outside the room, he told me of Grandma's grave illness and told me that she didn't recognize anyone.

"The doctors don't expect her to live for much longer, Emmy."

I nodded and choked back the tears, then went into the room to sit beside her. I took her hand in mine and said, "Hello, Grandma."

She looked at me and smiled. "Emmy, you came. Seeing you makes me so happy."

I just wanted to cry.

Then she said, "Emmy, I know the family called you evil, but you know, God loves you, and He knows you're not evil." Then she fell asleep.

How long I had waited to hear some loving words from someone in my family, and now she was dying.

As I prepared to leave, Uncle Dan walked out with me and did a good job of trying to burst my joy. "Don't believe anything she might have told you. In her state, she has no idea what she's saying."

"Uncle Dan, you can believe what you want, but I feel certain that she knew me and meant every word she told me." I paused a moment to look at him and said, "Thanks for all your support."

I left with tears in my eyes, and a great warmth in my heart. I felt so good about what she told me and felt certain that the message came from a higher power. Grandma died later that day. The following day I went to see Mom. She took me into the living room where the men from the funeral home had placed Grandma's body. They dressed Grandma in a new outfit that Mom had prepared for this occasion. Her body lay on a narrow table board, on the edge of the table.

I asked, "Isn't she going to fall off of that?" Mom said, "No, Emmy, she's very stiff and still."

When I touched her I understood. She looked peaceful, as if she slept. While Dad and the boys finished the casket Mom and I visited. I thought about telling her about what Grandma told me before she died but decided against it. I just kept it safe in my heart.

Chapter 6

A New Baby

Very pregnant now, I felt quite emotional. I feared having the baby. My memories of hearing the women scream while Mom helped them stayed close in my mind. I just wanted it all to go away. Spring finally arrived. As April came around, the weather got warmer and my mood improved. The baby moved around a lot and hurt my ribs. I couldn't seem to get comfortable.

On May third, about six in the evening, Carl and I played checkers at the dining room table when I felt a twinge different from any other ache or pain I had experienced. I looked at the clock and made a mental note of the time. The pain lasted about thirty seconds, and exactly fifteen minutes later I had another one. An hour later they came every ten minutes. After I had several more I told Carl about them and we decided that most likely they were labor pains.

I expected more pain than I felt. Soon I found out that they got more painful as time went on. By ten o'clock the pains arrived every five minutes and lasted longer and longer. We'd taken a class in Lamaze and I knew how to breathe and position myself for the most comfort. The doctor instructed me to wait to go to the hospital until my pains came every three minutes. About midnight I began to have nausea. Suddenly I had the urge to have a bowel movement and went to the toilet and while on the toilet I had to throw up. I felt horrible and wished I were in the hospital because I could hardly bear the pain. For a little while I just kept going to the bathroom and throwing up. I also noticed bloody discharge.

Carl tried to get a little sleep before he drove me to the hospital but I wanted to go, so I woke him up and we headed to Massena. After all the admission fuss and paperwork, they took me into a quiet, warm room where a nurse examined me.

She said, "Honey, you may as well go back home because you won't have this baby until tomorrow this time."

This shocked me, and I knew I couldn't do this for twenty-four hours. The pains came every one to two minutes and lasted a full minute, but we went back home.

At four o'clock I woke Carl up again and asked him to take me back. I couldn't take the pain any longer. The contractions got even more intense and lasted a minute-and-a-half. Sometimes they ran into each other and never stopped. Carl helped me get to the car. The Northern lights shone way up to the middle of the sky, not just streaks of light but a sky boiling with light. I thought the sight magnificent!

We returned to the hospital, hoping desperately they'd keep me and give me something for pain. Once there, they examined me and expressed surprise to find that my cervix had dilated quite a bit, but said I'd still have to wait a while. I thought maybe another hour. Wrong!

A different nurse arrived for duty, older and rough around the edges. She reminded me of Nurse Ratchet. She came into the room about every forty-five minutes and checked me.

One time she said, "It's time to break your water."

She left the room and came back with a big wooden stick that looked like a giant crochet hook. She pushed the hook inside me and snagged the lining of the uterus and broke it. Suddenly I felt warm water all over myself and then my pains got even worse. Sometimes I felt like I would just pass out.

I begged for something to deaden the pain, but they refused because they didn't want to deliver a groggy baby. Finally, they gave me a shot of something that helped a little. I got so tired I actually took tiny naps between contractions.

Finally, at about eleven o'clock the next morning I gave birth and I heard the doctor say, "It's a girl!"

They handed her to me. She looked like the most beautiful baby I had ever seen. She had beautiful pink skin and looked like a little China doll. Her eyes opened wide, and she looked all around. Now I just wanted to curl up and go to sleep. After they got me stitched up, they took the baby to perform all the newborn tests and pushed me to my room. Absolutely exhausted, I asked for a fruit juice. I took one sip and promptly went to sleep with the juice in my hand.

Sometime later one of the nurses tried to take the juice from my hand and it woke me up. I tried to move and felt something very wet and saw a pool of blood beneath me. I called for the nurse. They cleaned me up and immediately took me to a different department where they gave me two pints of blood. They didn't let me see the baby, even to nurse her, so my breasts got very full and hard. When I could finally nurse her it hurt so badly I almost cried. As I tried to feed the baby, I saw someone in the doorway. My mother!

She smiled, and she looked like Mom, not a "church member." I felt so happy to have her there that tears of joy came to my eyes and my heart felt very big and full. She helped me get the baby started nursing and we talked about what I wanted to name her.

I had two names picked out, Marilynn Rose and Leslie Ann. Carl didn't care which one I chose. As soon as I saw the baby I picked Marilynn Rose. I made it official that day. Mom and I enjoyed our visit, and I grew sad when she left. I hoped that maybe now that I had Marilynn, she'd visit on occasion and perhaps we could even be friends.

I continued to bleed at times but never needed more blood. After five days in the hospital they sent us home. Marilynn didn't cry much and she ate well and was so cute! My little family made me so happy. Carl's Mom and sisters helped. They sent flowers and came to see us on occasion, always bringing gifts. They had a baby shower for Marilynn and me. We got all kinds of little baby clothes and all the other things you need for a new baby.

Marilynn turned three weeks old, and I dressed her in a pretty pink dress with matching booties and had her picture taken at K-Mart in Massena. The photographer propped her up on a very pretty soft blanket and she looked up with her big blue eyes and smiled. I'd never seen a prettier baby!

Life went on. I didn't see much of my family. One day at the post office I ran into Amos Troyer.

I said, "Hello," and he just looked at me and walked the other way. I can't explain how that made me feel. I knew that I wasn't a bad person. They just didn't understand me.

I rarely went anywhere without little Marilynn. When Mother's Day's neared, a couple of weeks after Marilynn arrived, Carl wanted to take me to dinner with his Mom and Dad. I really didn't want to go and leave her but they planned it for only a couple of hours so I wouldn't have to miss a feeding. I agreed, and we went to a buffet in Winthrop.

All of the mothers got a red rose, and mine made me very proud. We had a good dinner then returned home. Kathy stayed home and watched after Marilynn.

At four weeks old, I noticed Marilynn had feet that were turned inward. When she tried to stand, they turned in so the soles faced each other and she stood on the outside of her feet. Dr. Dobies said that since she was a tall baby, her feet got positioned that way in the womb. He felt we could correct this if we started treatment at a very early age. At six weeks old, doctors placed casts on her legs, from toes to hips. She wore those until her legs outgrew them, then we put on a new set.

In June, Pam came out to spend the summer. I so enjoyed having Pam there. We went for walks and rides, and I liked having someone to talk with. We grew very close that summer. She helped me with makeup and clothes.

She also helped me with the English language. We grew up speaking Swiss, Dutch, and German in church. I learned to speak English in school, but found it difficult to use the language correctly. Pam and I also listened to a lot of music. I loved country music and Pam liked rock and roll, so we listened to some of each. She also spent some time with Mom and Dad that summer. Ben came over and picked her up and about a week later he brought her back. I missed them very much and prayed every day that they'd learn to accept me.

In the fall, Pam went back home and I began to make plans to go to Indiana for Christmas. I'd never flown on a plane so I got excited and a bit apprehensive. In September, Marilynn turned four months old and still wore casts on her legs. She'd grown big enough now to need the casts only up to her knees, which made her a lot easier to care for. She started weaning herself from nursing. I had no idea what happened, but one day she simply refused her afternoon feeding. When I tried to get her to eat she turned her little face away and screamed. She continued to cry until I gave her a bottle of milk. Another month went by and she refused another feeding. This went on until she had completely weaned herself. Her strong will amazed me.

In December, she and I went on our first plane ride. We got on a little commuter plane in Massena and flew to Syracuse. I feared the rough ride might make Marilynn sick, but she seemed okay. In Syracuse we taxied onto the runway then had to wait forty-five minutes to take off. She suddenly woke up and threw up all over me and everything around us. The flight attendant helped me clean up but for the rest of the flight I smelled vomit. I felt very bad for the other passengers who had to endure this.

We landed safely in Louisville, Kentucky, where Viola and the girls picked us up. Her home made me feel comfortable. I wanted to stay with them so badly, but didn't feel like I should leave Carl after he helped me so much. We had a wonderful Christmas and Viola tried to talk me into staying. They all described Carl as strange, but I felt very grateful to him for saving me. I didn't know why they thought him strange.

In the spring, I thought I'd like to go to work. I didn't know what I should try to do but just began to watch the ads in the paper. Carl had expanded on the shingle mill and put a sawmill in just down the road. After that, he bought a small trailer and built a room onto the side and we moved in.

We had little room, but had a place for a washer, dryer, and a family room. Soon after we moved in, I saw an ad in the paper for help at the new Ponderosa Steak House in Massena. I applied for a position and got it. My first real job!

A woman in Raymondville watched Marilynn for me and I started working part time in the afternoons and evenings. I mostly greeted people and took orders. I also helped cook some of the things and I carried food out to the people and cleaned up.

During the day I helped in the sawmill operating the front-end loader. This large, yellow and orange machine had a huge lift on the front. I loaded and unloaded trucks and stacked lumber. I also put the logs on the skids to the mill. I didn't mind helping out there and liked the work because I loved the outdoors.

Carl and I didn't do much together away from work. When he wasn't working he spent time with his buddies. I didn't think about it too much. I enjoyed spending time with Marilynn. He did take me out dancing on occasion. Painfully shy, I needed a couple of drinks before I'd dance. I loved music so when he got me started, I didn't want to stop. I wanted to learn as much as fast as I could. Sometimes when I drank, I wasn't a very nice person. At times I openly flirted with men who flirted with me. This made Carl very angry and on those occasions he called his Mom and talked about me in French.

I could understand that this wasn't appropriate behavior, but it didn't really matter to me. I didn't like that about myself and thought I should have more dedication to my marriage. One evening as we came home after I'd flirted with someone, he angrily threatened to drive the car off the road and kill us both. I started thinking then about what'd happened to us. I began to think about our relationship realistically. We'd never loved each other.

I had agreed to marry Carl because I had nowhere to live, no sense of belonging, no security. Marriage to him made it possible for me to not go back to the Amish.

I felt an incredible, deep sadness that seemed to fill every part of me. I knew at some point I needed to go out on my own because we couldn't fix this marriage. I also knew I never wanted to return to my family and that I must learn everything possible. I felt myself going into a depression.

Chapter 7

Separation

Marilynn kept me going. In the summer of 1980, I saw signs announcing a new store opening up in the little strip mall behind the Ponderosa. As soon as they began to take applications, I applied. I thought if I had a full time job somewhere, I'd make enough to support myself and Marilynn if I needed to. I prayed for direction every day and promised myself that I'd try to do everything I could to have a good marriage.

I went to the interview at Jamesway Department Store and left there with a new full-time job. I'd start in two weeks, working as a cashier. I went directly to Ponderosa and gave my two weeks' notice.

I enjoyed working at Jamesway. I had to change my schedule, but the same woman took care of Marilynn for me. I worked for two months and won a promotion to head cashier. I worked at the service desk, supervising the cashiers and keeping the registers tidy. Every day we had to count lots of money and it all had to come out even. I met some very nice people there. One woman, Bertha Olsen, a tiny elderly cashier, reminded me a lot of my mother. We talked a lot as she was the number one cashier. She'd worked as a cashier in other stores and had lots of good experience. She helped me so much. I had to work some weekends but usually only during the day.

The winter lasted a long time, and my spirits lifted when spring arrived. My supervisor asked me to go down state to help open a new store in Utica. After discussing it with Carl and making arrangements for Marilynn, I agreed to go. The first two days went as planned, then we got news of a big snowstorm coming in. We had a quick meeting and planned to leave a day earlier than we thought. It had already begun to snow when we left for home.

I didn't call to let Carl know of my early arrival. When I arrived near dawn. I got the shock of my life. I never knew what "gay" meant. People mentioned it to me several times. They thought Carl gay but I never gave it any thought. I just thought it meant that you were happy.

That morning as I let myself into our tiny home, right inside the door I saw another man's boots, coat and hat. I saw no one on the couch, or in the kitchen. One other room remained, the bedroom.

I listened closely and heard two people snoring. I stood frozen, not knowing what to do. My feet felt bolted to the floor. I couldn't move for what seemed like an eternity then I just very quietly walked back outside and left. I drove around for a while, stopped and had some coffee and when I thought everyone had gotten up and gone to work, I went home.

During that short time, I felt myself change. It's difficult to describe, but until that time I felt determined to make the marriage work. Now I really didn't care and prepared to move on. I didn't know how to tell Carl what I learned, so I just didn't tell him.

The next couple of days seemed awkward. I didn't feel like I belonged there but had no idea what to do or where to go. I tried to act normal around Carl because I feared what might happen if he knew. Doing nothing seemed like the thing for me to do at the time.

All this time I knew that I entered into the marriage for the wrong reasons but I thought Carl really cared about me. Now I knew that he used the marriage as a cover. I felt different. I looked in everyone's faces to see if I could get a sense of approval. I felt like I wasn't good enough or the right kind of person, and just when I started learning more about sex and my own sexuality, I find him in bed with a man. What did that say about me? I must have something dreadfully wrong with me. I began to flirt with men again and the men that I saw worked in our sawmill. They flirted back, which seemed like approval to me.

A couple months went by and I got a raise at work. I talked with several women who raised their children alone, and decided to talk with Carl and explain that I wanted my own place. I can't really remember the exact time I talked with him, but he told me if I didn't want to stay with him, he didn't want anything to do with me or Marilynn. We dropped it and some time later he told me that he'd help me find an apartment. We found a trailer park near Massena that had a trailer for rent. We rented it, and I took a few dishes and a little of this and that. Carl let me take the stereo which pleased me so much, and he said I could have the green car and he'd keep the truck.

The first time Marilynn and I went to church after our

separation, I felt very strange. Although Carl never went to church with us it just seemed strange to me. Marilynn and I went to church with Jody and her family, a little Methodist church in Raymondville. Jody and I sang in the choir and Marilynn, age two, sat with one of the women during my choir duties.

After the separation, she began to cling to me. One Sunday we had services in the basement to save on energy as it was very cold. Marilynn sat in her own little rocking chair while I sang. After I went up to the choir she decided she wanted to go with me and from the back row of the church she dragged the rocking chair across the concrete floor and put it up there next to me and sat there very pretty while we finished the song. The entire church laughed!

Everyone knew her as a good baby, always happy, and one who listened well most of the time. I felt very strange in church that day. Because Carl and I split, I feared the Lord's unhappiness on my head. I felt so bad that I decided not to go back to church again.

That certainly turned out to be a big mistake. I could feel myself becoming someone I didn't know. I don't think I wanted to feel this way, but I couldn't help it. After Marilynn and I moved out on our own I took her back home almost every evening to see her father. I encouraged him to take her for weekends but he refused, still saying that he didn't want her without me.

This tore me in two. I felt I was wrong to leave, yet I didn't think he really wanted me for the right reasons. Some time passed and I went to the movies with a date. He kissed me and left a hickey on my neck. This made me furious and I never spoke to him again.

The following day when I took Marilynn to see her father he saw it and got even more furious. He yelled at me and called me names. That's when I finally had the nerve to tell him that I came home early and found him with a friend in his bed.

After a few moments of silence he blurted out, "When I get to the pearly gates, I'll tell God I'm no queer."

With that he turned around, got in his truck and drove away. I think me knowing this about him made him very nervous. The only male child in a proud, French Canadian family, he didn't want his Mom and Dad to know about his other life. He searched for ways to discredit me to them.

Up until this time he had absolutely no intent of spending time with Marilynn except when I brought her around. I asked him several times if he'd like to have her spend the weekend with him and he never wanted to. That's why his presence at my door the next Saturday morning surprised me.

"Could I take Marilynn for the weekend?" he asked. "I'd like to spend the weekend with my parents and they'd really like to see her."

Excited, I got her ready and sent her with her father for the weekend. I had to work all weekend and asked him to bring her home on Sunday evening by four o'clock. He said yes, and they left. Pam, who came for a visit, could be available when he brought Marilynn home. When Carl didn't return Marilynn as planned, Pam rushed back to where I worked and told me. Immediately I got a terrible fear in the pit of my stomach.

I spoke with my manager who arranged to let me leave and Pam and I drove to Carl's parents' house together.

When we arrived, Carl and his parents sat around the kitchen table and as usual I just walked in. They had large sliding glass doors that you could see through from the driveway. I stepped inside and saw Marilynn come running out of the bedroom to see me.

Very quickly, his Dad came over and hit me on my right shoulder and threw me out the door. I landed on the concrete. He then slammed the door and locked it. I could see Marilynn crying and trying to get to me. Kathy came and picked her up and took her back into the bedroom. I tried to talk with Carl through the door but he just shook his head and turned the other way.

Pam got my attention and said, "Come on, Emma, we have to go home and call Mom."

So we went home and called Viola. She advised me to find an attorney in the morning and she'd wire money if we needed it. I didn't sleep at all that night. I couldn't believe he had really taken my baby away from me after he said he didn't want anything to do with her. All night I kept seeing Marilynn's little face as she ran toward me then the look on her face when someone snatched her away from me. I could hear her crying. It was a living nightmare.

Finally, Monday morning arrived and Pam and I went to Canton in search of an attorney. We looked through the phone book and called several people. We finally found one named Harold Smith who could see us immediately.

I felt comfortable with Harold Smith and told him the story.

"Okay, I need a retainer of $500," he said. "I'll write up an affidavit asking for temporary custody."

We called Viola and she wired the money. Mr. Smith

wrote the papers and had them delivered appropriately. Carl very quickly retained an attorney named Jones, probably in his thirties and very cocky. They scheduled a court appearance for four days later. This seemed like the longest time in the world to me, and I felt very frightened.

First of all, I had never set foot in a courtroom. I didn't know anything about how the system worked and so I had no idea what to expect. Secondly, I knew Carl and his family had enough money to do whatever they pleased. Everyone knew and respected them. No one knew me, a little nobody who'd run away from home.

When the day came to go to court, I felt a little better but still so frightened I had a hard time functioning properly. When I tried to talk I got tongue-tied and the words wouldn't come out right. I just kept thinking, surely no one wanted to take a baby away from her mother. I felt the judge would know that what had happened was wrong.

When we walked into the courtroom, my entire body trembled. Mr. Smith took my arm and walked in with me. Carl and Mr. Jones looked very smug. The attorneys went through the opening comments then Mr. Jones attacked me. He told the judge that I had no idea about how a wife and mother should act. He accused me of sleeping with Carl's staff at the mill and tried to discredit me very quickly.

At the end of that day, the judge awarded temporary custody to me. When he told me that I could go get Marilynn I felt so happy. I missed her so much and I knew she missed me as well. We had never stayed apart for very long. I got in the car with Pam and just cried and cried. We had to have an escort from the sheriff's department present to pick her up. He walked into the house and she came out holding his hand. She walked with him all the way to the road where we picked her up. I wasn't allowed in their driveway.

We left as quickly as we could. The court set a date for custody hearings. The judge told both of us that we should not have Marilynn around other people, meaning people of the opposite sex. I had no intention of dating anyone. However, some of the people I worked with, male and female, came over to see us. We all sat down and played a game of cards. The next day I received a notice to appear in court for having Marilynn around another man. I had no idea it meant any and all males. The man at our house arrived with his girlfriend.

The judge admonished me and I felt too shy to ask questions or try to explain what happened. Mr. Smith, helpful and encouraging, asked me to get in touch with my family and ask if anyone could come to testify in my behalf. He thought they could testify that I had the ability to take care of Marilynn, and to let the court know that I had taken care of many children in my life.

I gathered my courage and went home. I saw Mom and Dad and some of my brothers. We visited for a few minutes. I left Marilynn with Pam because I wasn't sure how they'd act and I didn't want to frighten Marilynn. I caught them by surprise so they didn't have the opportunity to form a plan to hold me. I sensed, however, that the boys had a plan forming.

They all went outside while I talked with Mom and then started filing in through the back door. I left instructions with Pam to come look for me if I wasn't back in two hours. At this point I opened the subject of the custody and quickly explained my needs. I told them that I knew no one else to testify on my behalf. I said they needn't approve of my lifestyle, but just needed to describe me as a competent person and a good mother.

I believe my mother wanted to help, but Pete spoke up. "We can't and won't help you in your evil ways. The whole court system is evil, and the church will not allow us to associate with it."

I felt as if someone had just ripped out my heart. Standing in the kitchen with Mom and the boys, I looked around. Pete glared at me and the other boys looked at their shoes.

With tears in her eyes, Mom said to Pete, "You don't think we could help her keep her baby?"

Pete said, "No." He had a smirk on his face and a chew of tobacco in his mouth. I think I almost hated him.

"But, with the Lord's will and grace, anything's possible."

"Pete, you tell me why going into the courthouse is evil," I demanded.

"We can't help you while you continue to disobey the rules of the church, but I'll make a deal with you. If you agree to live at home and raise Marilynn in the Amish church, we'll help you. We'll go to court and testify for you. We'll do whatever you need, but you have to agree to this in front of the church and God. And as long as Carl lives, you can never remarry, because the Amish church does not recognize divorce."

"First you didn't recognize my marriage, in fact you called me an adulteress. You didn't recognize my child when she was born, now you say you won't recognize my divorce. How can there even be a divorce if there's no marriage. None of this makes any sense."

"Those are words from the devil," Pete said folding his arms across his chest.

"I can see that no matter what I say, you'll never change your mind, and no matter what you say, you'll never change mine." I turned to leave.

Dad barred my way and pointed his finger at me. "You now live an evil, God forsaken, devil-worshiping life, that's why you have all these problems. Very soon you'll burn in hell forever and ever."

Tears welled in my eyes but I held them back. All the way home I wished I had never gone. Getting home to Marilynn and Pam felt like such a relief. I picked Marilynn up and hugged her until she begged for me to put her down. As tired as I was that night, I hated to go to sleep because I still had nightmares about Dad and other members of my family kidnapping me. But I had to get on with my life.

CHCHCH

The next day I went to work with my head spinning. I didn't know what to do. I suspected everyone. I looked out the window and saw Carl's truck pull into the far entrance to the store parking lot and he parked way out at the end. I saw someone get out of the passenger side. I couldn't see who, but it frightened me and I didn't know what to do. I decided to walk out with someone when I left work.

I walked out with Frank who worked in receiving. He stood over six feet tall and weighed about three hundred pounds. Although gentle, he looked scary. I couldn't see

Carl's truck anymore and felt relieved, but when I got to my car I found two flat tires. I had only one spare tire in my trunk. Frank offered to take me home and bring another tire the next day. I accepted and when we pulled into my driveway, I saw Carl's truck on the other side of the road. He sat watching me.

The next day I received another subpoena to go to court for having a man at my house. Frank didn't even come in my house. He dropped me off outside. Marilynn, inside the apartment, didn't even see him or know that he gave me a ride home. I couldn't win, no matter what I did. He had more power, more money, more influence. Even through all of this I never really believed that I'd lose my baby.

Chapter 8

A New Home

I'd looked in the paper for a less expensive apartment to rent. With all the court expense I wanted to pay less in rent. I saw an ad for an apartment close to where I lived and went to look at it. Located about a half mile up the road, I found it; a two-story house separated into four apartments, two upstairs and two downstairs, with the available one upstairs. I liked the one-bedroom apartment and decided to take it. A small diner sat across the street. Our friends, Pat and Shirley, owned it and we frequently spent time there. We moved into the new apartment about the first week of July.

About a week later someone knocked on the door and there stood Ben. When I opened the door to let him in I heard a rumble and looked behind him. Up the stairway and into the apartment barged three more of my brothers.

"What's going on, Ben?"

"Don't get upset, Emmy. The boys just want to talk to you."

While Ben tried to reassure me, my brothers positioned themselves around the apartment; one at the door and the other three surrounding me.

One of them said, "We don't plan to leave without you."

I had no idea what to do. I didn't have a phone and Pam wasn't there. I talked with them for a while and didn't get anywhere.

Then one brother said, "Mom's not feeling well. You need to stop playing games and come home. She needs you."

"That's not going to work. You tried that before. You're really going to have to get more creative."

"Emmy, please, you've got to come home with us. We all need you."

"I'm not going with you, and that's the end of it. Now, you can all stay here and stare at each other if you'd like, but I'm tired. It's been a long day. I'm going to bed."

One of my brothers stood at my bedroom door. "I can't allow you to go in there."

"What? Are you nuts? We're on the second floor. Do you think I would jump out the window?"

He stood with his feet apart and arms folded over his chest.

I lost it and started throwing things around the apartment. "Here, Ben, you want to read a book?" I threw it at him. He ducked just before it whizzed past where his head had been.

"Pete, how about some flowers?" I threw a vase with silk flowers at him.

"Life's a bitch!" I screamed and jumped up and down on the couch.

They all looked at one another and left. I breathed a

sigh of relief and sank onto the couch in a puddle of tears. How could my own brothers do this to me?

Pam arrived as they cleared the bottom of the stairs from my door.

"Who were they and…what happened here?" she asked as she looked around my usually tidy apartment.

I told her the whole story and she held me as I wept on her shoulder.

"Take it easy, Emmy. It'll be okay. We won't let anyone take you or Marilynn. We'll keep you safe."

The next day as I came home from work a police officer met me in the driveway.

"Ma'am could I come up and search your apartment?" he asked.

"Why, what have I done?"

"Well, ma'am, you brothers came by the station and said that last night you took something out of the kitchen cabinet and suddenly started acting very crazy. They said they thought you had taken some sort of drug."

"Officer, did he tell you why I was acting crazy? I was fighting for my survival. They wanted to kidnap me and take me back home." Then I told him the whole story.

The officer shook his head in disbelief. "Sorry, Ma'am. Here's my card if you have any other problems." He turned and left.

I closed the door behind me and sank to the floor. I wished for one day with a little peace. I thought about my mother a lot and wished her well. I missed her very much, but if my family was going to act like this, she could never be a part of my life.

We had a couple of quiet days, which I welcomed.

Marilynn wanted a kitten and I saw an ad in the paper for free kittens. Marilynn and I went to look at them and found two white ones we liked. I got a litter box and food at work that day. When we got home she played and played with the kittens. She had a hard time going to sleep because she wanted them to sleep with her..

I spent a lot of time talking with Mr. Smith about the impending court proceedings. He tried to prepare me for the custody case, but I never expected the viciousness that I saw.

During the first couple of days the judge tried to get testimony from everyone. Mr. Jones subpoenaed all the men that I worked with and the men who worked at Carl's sawmill. I walked into the courthouse to see a hall lined with men. He accused me of having an affair with each one. Although I didn't have an affair, it greatly humiliated me.

The next day I prepared to go to court when I looked out my window just in time to see Carl run up to the house and take the license plate off my car and quickly drive away. I knew I'd get in trouble if I drove it without a license plate so I borrowed a friend's car and drove to court. I sat in the hallway waiting to get called in when a deputy sheriff came to me and asked me to go to the department with him.

"What for?" I asked.

"Ma'am, we have reason to believe that you drove an unlicensed vehicle and we have to arrest you."

I told him what happened and that I didn't drive the car, so he couldn't arrest me. "So now are you going to arrest Carl for the theft of the plates?"

"No, ma'am. It's his car."

"But he gave it to me."

"It doesn't matter," the sheriff explained. "The car is in his name."

When I explained all this to the judge that day, the judge ordered Carl to furnish me with another car of equal value, in my name.

On this count, Carl did comply. He bought me a huge, baby blue station wagon. When I drove it to my next court date, I became very ill with a horrible headache. I had to get to court on time, so I didn't stop. Then I saw an officer behind me trying to get me to pull over.

What now? I thought as I pulled over. Everything looked blurry and the road seemed to move in front of me. The officer came up to my side of the car. He opened the door and pulled me out. He began to talk to me and made me walk up and down the road with him. Then he called a tow truck, helped me into his car and took me on to court.

They took the car to a garage and determined that someone had tampered with it to make fumes go inside the car. They couldn't say that Carl did it because he'd just bought the car and said he didn't know about it. I knew better. I felt certain he did this on purpose, and wanted me dead.

Court exhausted me. Every day something else happened, and Carl had people testifying in his behalf. Even his elementary schoolteacher and the principle from the high school came in to testify.

Viola testified on my behalf and told how I helped other mothers with newborns. I also blessed her for saying that I was a very capable mother and could care well for

Marilynn.

The garage repaired the car and brought it to me, and again, life quieted for a few days. I worked on weekends so I could go to court during the day. I also worked some at night to make enough money to pay the rent and get food.

The week after the incident with the car, Pam said that Allie and Debbie wanted to come over to play cards one evening. This sounded good to me. The next day, Wednesday, I had off from work and from court. Their mothers owned the diner across the road so Pam went over to ask them.

I noticed the neighbor going up and down the stairs with boxes of stuff. When I had a chance, I asked if she was leaving. She didn't stop or make eye contact with me but just said, "No, I'm spending the night with my mom."

I thought that a bit strange because I saw that she carried a box with a blender in it. I decided to mind my own business and just put it out of my mind.

We had dinner and Allie and Debbie came over and we played Eucker, a card game for four people, and had a great time. We stayed up until one o'clock. Marilynn fell asleep on the couch with the kittens so I picked her up and put her in her crib and went to bed. Pam slept on the cot in the family room. That night felt very warm, and I took off my wedding ring and put it on the floor, which I'd done before. I'd decided to wear them until divorced. The bed sat on a tiny frame with only a box spring and a mattress. Exhausted, I fell asleep immediately.

At about four o'clock I woke suddenly because of noises downstairs. I thought maybe Mom had gotten worse and my family had come for me, so I jumped up and ran to the window. I immediately saw bright orange and red flames shooting out into the darkness, coming from the window next to me. I looked around me and saw smoke rolling in from everywhere. I suddenly realized that it was very hot. I ran straight to Marilynn's bed and picked her up. She woke up and looked at me but never said a word. I buried her face in my chest and told her to hold on tight just like that. She did exactly as I said and never moved.

We hurried into the family room where Pam slept on the couch. I feared she wouldn't wake up because she slept so heavily, but she got up instantly. I told her the house is on fire and we must get out immediately. She grabbed her wallet and we made it to the door. The smoke had filled the apartment by now and I felt very frightened.

The door to the apartment had a lock that opened only with a key and we generally kept the key hanging beside the door. It wasn't there. We could hardly talk or breathe now for the smoke, but I asked Pam about the key. Without a word she reached over to the top of the stereo, which we could hardly see for the smoke, and came back with the key. She unlocked the door and we stepped out into the enclosed stairway that went to the parking lot, by now totally filled with smoke. We held onto each other and finally made it to the bottom. We coughed so hard that we could barely breathe.

As we walked away from the building I heard a loud crash behind us. I looked back and saw the window that I looked out of only a few minutes earlier blow out and hit the ground behind us. I realized then how lucky we'd been to have gotten out of the apartment alive. I felt a great warmth come over me because I knew in my heart that the

Lord loved me and took care of me.

I found out that the noise I heard earlier came from the people downstairs moving their furniture out. We got out to the middle of the parking lot when Carl drove in. A few minutes after that, the fire trucks arrived. I wondered how Carl knew about the fire and got there so fast, even before the fire trucks, but quickly forgot about it and thought about what to do to take care of us. The three of us stood out there with nothing but our nightclothes on. Some of the neighbors offered to give me a housecoat which I gladly accepted.

Carl came over and asked, "How'd you make it out so fast, Emma?"

Stunned, I just stared at him.

"Well, now you have no choice. You have to come back home."

My mind raced and every breath pained my lungs. I knew that I'd never go home with him. I believed he tried to kill us. Someone brought me a pair of jeans with a hole in the right knee and a flannel shirt. I put them on and Uncle Rob came driving in and said he'd like to take us to get some breakfast. We got in the truck and went to a little breakfast place in Norwood.

I felt like a fog had enveloped me, but somehow between coughs I choked down an egg and hash browns. We went back to the apartment saw the entire house had burned. My car, parked next to it, had burned as well.

I knew I had some things to take care of that day and needed a car. Pam and I talked about it and decided to borrow Carl's truck for the day. We took Marilynn and went to Jamesway department store. I knew that I could get us a toothbrush and Marilynn something to wear because I worked there. I didn't have any money because my purse burned. I lived totally check to check and didn't have a bank account. Now we had nothing but the clothes we wore. Ed, our security manager, always arrived early to open the store. I wanted to get there before the store opened to the public.

I knocked on the door and he let us in. I told him what happened and he told me to find whatever we need and bring the tickets to him. I got each of us a pair of shoes, an outfit, underwear, toothbrush, and toothpaste. I brought him all the tags and he gave me a big hug then tore the tags up and threw them in the trash.

Still in shock, I didn't realize all of what happened but when he displayed that kindness and generosity it hit me that I had friends, people who cared about me. I broke down and cried. We got dressed there then went to Canton to the Social Services Department. I thought I could get some assistance there, maybe help with a vehicle, a place to stay for a week or so.

I spoke with three people before they directed me to the right one. He asked me to fill out numerous papers and bring them back to him. It seemed like it took forever to fill out all the papers but finally, I finished and returned them to him. He looked at me and said I'd get notice by mail in six to eight weeks to let me know if I qualified for any assistance.

"Six to eight weeks? I need a place for us to stay tonight! My niece and two-year old daughter are with me. Where are we going to stay?

He looked at me and said, "What do you think we are

back here, moneybags?"

I couldn't believe what I heard. He had a very stern look on his face so without another word I turned around and walked away. As I tried to get out of the building I walked straight into a glass door. I bounced back, quickly realized what happened, went back to the door, opened it and walked through. I felt like an orphan child with nowhere to go. I felt dirty, hungry, tired, and weak, and my lungs burned.

I got back to the truck where Pam and Marilynn waited and quickly cheered up. I didn't want Marilynn to see me feeling bad. We drove back to Massena and went to the little diner across the road from the apartment. We went in and sat down. Pat was working and brought us some French fries and drinks.

"Thanks, Pat, but I have absolutely no money," I said.

She stood with her hand on her hip. "No money, huh? Good. Just take this as a gift," and she gave us all a big hug.

"So do you have a place to stay?" Pat asked.

"No, nowhere."

"I have a little log cabin in the woods behind the diner. You can stay there for a couple of months if you want. There's no running water and little furniture, but it's got a roof and walls."

Again, I felt that lump of emotion in my throat. Someone else cared about us. We graciously accepted, then walked back to take a look.

Old and small, it sat back in the woods. Even when the sun shone, it didn't reach there. It had two beds, an old couch, a couple of chairs, and a table. The doors didn't lock well and that worried me.

While the girls stayed at the cabin, I walked back to the diner and called my attorney with news of the day's activity. I also told him about the girl next door moving all her stuff out the night before and said that I suspected that Carl started the fire. He advised me to act with extreme care and stay alert at all times.

I didn't have a car so until I got a check, I hitchhiked to work and back. After I got my check I took a cab. The first couple of nights in the cabin, I got very scared. I hardly slept for fear of Carl pulling something else. I kept a paring knife under my pillow at all times. We stacked two chairs in front of the door because of the bad lock. Pam slept in the little bedroom, which seemed like a long way from my room.

Day and night, darkness enveloped the cabin. I couldn't identify the noises outside, and at one point I got frightened enough to ask Pam to stay in my bedroom. Frightened too, she crawled across the floor to my bedroom. Marilynn slept soundly and had no idea about all the noises going on outside. Needless to say, I didn't get much sleep that night.

I went to work the next day and had a difficult time keeping my mind on work because I worried so about Marilynn and Pam. I couldn't call them because we had no phone. As I prepared to call a cab to go home, one of the store managers gave me a certificate for a hundred dollars in merchandise from the store. The employees all gave to a fund and that came to a hundred and sixty dollars, so I received a total of $240.

Overwhelmed, I started crying and couldn't stop. I felt

so grateful for these people. They didn't really know me but treated me with so much kindness. I felt like I had a family right there at work.

With the money I bought a cast iron skillet. I didn't know to "season" it first, so I fried some eggs and they tasted horrible! I didn't know why but mentioned it to one of my friends. She informed me of the need to season the frying pan before using it, and told me how. After I did this, everything tasted great.

Every night it seemed a little less scary but we continued to hear noises outside that sounded like someone or something, probably animals, walking in the dry leaves. One evening a young woman with a backpack knocked on our door. She looked distressed and frightened. I felt sympathetic and opened the door.

"Hi, I'm Christy," she offered me her hand. "I was staying in a cabin down the road and didn't like staying there by myself."

I invited her in.

She began to tell me her story. She said she accidentally ran over her boyfriend's dog in Buffalo, and that he got angry and she ran off. Her father feared her boyfriend, too, and sent her away for a couple of weeks until the boyfriend cooled off. She asked permission to sleep on our floor. Pam and I agreed. We disliked living alone, too, and we liked helping someone.

She made friends with Marilynn very quickly, as well as the rest of us. The next morning she asked me how I get to work and offered to drive me there and pick me up to pay back for letting her stay there. That seemed like a good deal for me and so she gave me a ride to work and later came back and picked me up.

She insisted on stopping at Burger King and buying burgers and fries for our dinner, also to pay us back. We didn't get to eat fast food much because we couldn't afford it. All in all, we liked having Christy with us.

Chapter 9

Back to Court

After a break, we headed back to court the next week. I dreaded going back because of all that had happened during the last session. However, I prayed a lot and talked to myself and just pulled up those bootstraps and went forward.

The day before we went back, Carl came to the cabin. He acted friendly and pleasant, and I introduced him to Christy. He asked me if he could talk with me in private. We went outside and he told me that he'd forget everything and give me a divorce if I promised not to ask for child support. I knew he didn't really want Marilynn, but apparently he also didn't want any responsibilities. I told him that I'd only speak to my attorney about child support. Angry, he started yelling. I calmly turned around and went back into the house and locked the door.

When court began, Christy disappeared. I assumed she'd returned home. Viola testified for me, the only person who did. On the last day of court as my attorney and I walked in, I saw Christy sitting with Carl and his attorney. This shocked me. I realized they'd set me up and they planned to have her testify against me. My attorney asked for a recess and we got up and went outside. I told him all that I could think of and we went back inside.

Sure enough, Christy testified against me. She told the court that I fed Marilynn raw hot dogs and that she brought fast food to our house to make sure the baby got food. She also said I drank alcohol in front of Marilynn, but the only alcohol coming into the cabin, beer, Christy brought in.

She told a whole litany of lies which I can't remember. As she talked, my attorney took notes and I helped him. When he questioned her, he addressed everything she said. Because of her youth and inexperience, he caught her in several lies. She broke down in tears and pointed to Carl.

"He paid me to say those things."

"Young lady, don't you realize that people's lives hang in the balance here? You should be ashamed of yourself. Now, get off the stand. I admonish you to think about what you've done and do better."

My attorney said, "Your Honor, in view of this witness' testimony, I move that it be striken from the record."

"Mr. Smith, I will take her testimony lightly but I cannot strike it entirely."

I felt very dazed and confused and for the first time I thought I might lose Marilynn. The court proceedings soon ended, so now we waited for the judge to decide who got custody. They told me we'd know in about two weeks.

Pam prepared to return to Indiana for school. I took her to the airport and a couple days later Viola came to stay with me again, which pleased and relieved me.

I needed a car and watched the ads in the paper for

something I could afford. I found an ad for an old Maverick for two hundred dollars. I went to the little bank in our parking lot and the man there gave me a ninety-day note. I felt so proud to buy that car. Next, Viola and I looked for an apartment in town and found one that I could afford.

Two weeks came and went and still no word from the judge. Viola took care of Marilynn while I worked. She dropped me off at work and picked me up in the evening. While I worked, she and Marilynn went to the park or to yard sales. They had lots of adventures to tell me about.

Meanwhile, I wondered why the judge took so long in making his decision. Viola said he had a lot of information to consider. Each time I called the attorney's office, I got the same answer: "We should hear something soon."

Soon a month had passed and we still had no word. Part of me felt good about it, and part felt frightened. I simply could not imagine Marilynn not living with me. I had no other family now, and I didn't know how to go on if they took her away from me.

Six weeks passed and still no word. Viola and I talked about it and I decided to contact the bar association for the state of New York. This took work, with numerous papers to fill out and a written narrative about the case. Next, we waited on both the judge's decision and the bar association's investigation. After two months passed I told my attorney I planned to contact the media if I didn't hear something soon.

A few days later we got the answer. Viola came to pick me up from work by herself. I knew something had happened when I didn't see Marilynn's face in the window, waving and jumping up and down as usual. Then I saw the look on Viola's face, and her tears.

Every inch of me seemed to melt away. I whispered, "Where's Marilynn?"

She said, "They came and took her and I couldn't stop them."

Numb, we said little as we drove back to the apartment. I felt unable to focus on anything. I reached for the handle on the car door and couldn't even grasp it. Back in the apartment, I looked around me and saw signs of Marilynn everywhere. Her little tricycle sat there. I stared at it.

The next day I went to see my attorney. He'd told me to bring Marilynn to his office, but Viola and I went by ourselves. After we parked the car, and walked down the sidewalk, I started to get really angry. It boiled up inside. When we got inside, I didn't act as I had before, the quiet, sweet, submissive, patient, and forgiving person. I realized, suddenly, the unfairness of life. They cheated, and they took my baby away from me.

My attorney hugged me. Then he said, "I guess they have her."

I nodded.

Carl's Mom got custody of Marilynn and I got weekend visitation. The judge deemed Carl an unfit parent and denied him custody. He didn't give me custody because he felt that Carl wouldn't stop trying to hurt us, putting both Marilynn's safety and mine at risk.

I don't remember leaving the office that day and I don't remember the next couple of days. I remember getting Marilynn for visitation, and I remember she thought she'd come home to stay. When I took her back she cried and held onto me begging me not to leave her. I could sense that this arrangement wouldn't work for us. She wasn't old enough to understand and felt torn every time.

The judge said he felt certain that I'd want to seek custody again at a later date. I wondered what he meant. Then the bar's report on its investigation came through. It said that both the judge and Mr. Jones would not be able to continue to practice in the State of New York.

"Does that make any difference in the decision about Marilynn?" I asked my attorney.

He shook his head. "Unfortunately, no."

I thought about reopening the case but found myself financially and emotionally depleted. Viola helped me as much as she could, but she didn't have much herself at the time.

As Viola prepared to go home, I decided to go with her. I feared staying there by myself. I sold my little car, bought a station wagon, loaded it up and headed down the highway. Putting the hurt and pain behind me felt good. I missed Marilynn very much and I focused on how to get her back.

As we drove toward Indiana, everything hit me. Viola had to drive. I cried and cried, then I slept for a long time. I had no energy. I felt empty and very tired. We arrived at Viola's house the end of October. I can't remember those days very well, but do recall them as never-ending. Shortly after this, I learned that the judge had died following a massive heart attack.

I walked in the woods and wrote in my journal. I wrote down my feelings, hoping I'd feel better after writing. I called Marilynn every weekend. We talked very little because of her age, two-and-a-half. She didn't want to talk on the phone and many times she didn't. But I kept calling. As she grew older, we talked more.

I found a part-time job at a Kroger's Supermarket. I enjoyed it a lot because I got to interact with people. I enjoyed and appreciated living with Viola and Charlie, who treated me like a part of the family. The girls and I felt like sisters. They were several years younger than me and had their own friends, but always made me feel welcome.

Viola cooked a big dinner for Thanksgiving and invited some of her good friends over, including Gayle Ralston whose wife had died several years earlier. Gayle and his family continued to visit, and he brought his son Walter, nicknamed Bim, to dinner.

Bim had just left the Army after eight years and had gotten a divorce recently. We talked about his family for hours and seemed to have much in common. We made plans to get together again, and I felt excited about seeing him. I started thinking about trying to get Marilynn back if I found a suitable man to marry. The judge had told me he felt I was a good parent but had lots of things working against me. He encouraged me to apply again for custody when I had had a more stable life. This stayed in my head.

Bim seemed to understand how I felt about Marilynn as he had just lost custody of his three daughters. We began to see each other on a regular basis and I got very attached to him. Viola encouraged me to go to college and make something of my life. I remember one day in particular that she practically begged me to take advantage of this time without responsibility to get an education. But I placed more importance on safety and security, which I felt with

Bim. Stepping out on my own to do anything seemed out of the question. Thinking about college and living by myself frightened me.

I stayed in touch with Marilynn on a weekly basis. I got visitation over Christmas that year and arranged for us to stay with Bertha Olsen. She lived in the country with her husband and had two policeman sons living nearby. I felt safe staying there. I called ahead and arranged to pick Marilynn up. I drove in snow and ice, and getting there took me twenty-four hours. But seeing her, finally, made me so happy.

I walked up to the door and she came running. I'd wondered if she'd know me and want to come with me. After all, it had been two months since I had seen her. I picked her up and she hugged me tight. It made me so happy to feel her hug me back. Her grandmother had her bags packed and we put them in the car and took off.

I thought about running away with her, but I knew they'd find us and then prevent me from seeing her again, so I just drove over to Bertha's house. She had a room ready for us to stay in. What a good friend!

We got to spend two weeks together. We didn't go outdoors much because of the cold. The temperature went down to 48 degrees below zero and stayed at 30 degrees below zero for a whole week. So we played indoor games and did other activities. All too soon my two weeks ended and I headed back to Indiana. I cried for days at leaving Marilynn behind. After I got home and went back to work, life went on.

My mother always said, "Time can heal everything." This hurt seemed to go on and on.

Several weeks after my return I saw an ad in the paper for a full-time position at a new Swifty Food and Gas Mart opening in town. I applied and got the position. As I worked more, I felt less sorry for myself. I still called Marilynn every week and began to make plans to go see her the following summer. I also continued to see Bim.

He took a job with a construction company building and reconstructing cooling towers and began to travel often. After some time we broke up and once again Viola tried to convince me to go to school. But I thought only of stabilizing my life, as the judge had said, so I could get Marilynn back. At the time, college didn't seem like the right thing for me. I had absolutely no interest in an education.

That summer, 1981, Viola, Pam, Perry (Viola's grandson), and I got in the van and drove to New York to pick Marilynn up for the summer. We called ahead and made an appointment with her grandmother. When we arrived she remembered me and seemed happy to see me. I picked her up and she hugged me tight. She'd grown tall now and felt heavy.

At three years old she had a great vocabulary. I don't think she stopped talking for several hours! Seeing her made me so happy, and her beauty and intelligence overwhelmed me so, I almost couldn't speak. She awed me.

I wanted to see my family while there. My sister wrote me that Mom had colon cancer, had surgery in the fall, and improved. I wrote back and let her know when I'd come and said I wanted to see Mom. I made a mistake telling them my schedule. It never occurred to me that, even now, they'd try to hold me captive.

We drove into the driveway and everything looked calm. Pam and I went to the door and Viola took Marilynn and Perry to the outhouse. We walked into the house and to my great surprise I saw all my sisters, sister-in-laws, nieces, and nephews! I immediately wondered how they got there because I didn't see any buggies when we pulled in. After saying hello I looked around and the back door opened and all the brothers filed in. At this point I knew what they planned.

I looked at Pam and we passed a silent message to each other. She could see it, too, and began to slowly inch her way to the front door. I continued to chat and tried to keep my wits about me. I stood in the center of the room with a view to both the front and back door. Very soon the boys surrounded me.

I gave a desperate look to Pam and she said, "Emmy, we should really go." She reached for the front door and opened it quickly.

Before the boys could stop her she stood in the doorway. One of them pushed her out and closed the door. As I saw this happening I quickly ran out the back door hoping to get out through the garage.

I heard someone say, "She's going out the back!"

I heard them behind me and ran as fast as I could. I wasn't fast enough, however, because as I ran through the garage door Ben met me from the front and he picked me up.

Very soon the rest of the family surrounded me. The boys stood in a circle and held me by my arms, legs, and wherever they could. I dangled in mid air. I kicked, screamed and bit, but they wouldn't let go. I called to Pam to go get the cops and she ran for the van. One of the boys ran after her but she ran faster and jumped in and took off, leaving a cloud of dust.

I calmed down. When Pam returned with the cops, they'd set me free. I wasn't angry with my family because I knew they saw what they did as saving me from the devil. I understood that they didn't want to harm me, but the repeated scene and their feelings about me and my evil ways disappointed me.

Dad walked up to me while the boys had me hanging in mid air. He had a captive audience. "You need to think about changing your ways and coming back to the church. If only you'd come home and make your peace with the church, you'd have a chance at seeing the kingdom of heaven."

"Why can't you let me be?" I screamed at him.

"Unless you come home and change your ways, you'll most certainly burn in hell for ever and ever. It's my job as your father to make sure that doesn't happen."

He didn't hear well, so I shouted very loudly, "Pam went to get the police, so you should tell the boys to put me down and turn me loose."

He looked long and hard at me then turned and walked away. As he walked off he said, "Put her down, boys." He never looked back or said anything else to me.

The boys put me down and very soon Pam returned with the police right behind her. I told them very quickly what happened and that my family freed me. The police drove away and I got in the van and we left as well.

As we drove away I looked back and saw my mother fall to the ground. At first I thought the van hit her so we stopped. She immediately got up and seemed okay. I felt very bad for her and wished I could do something to help her. I knew she missed me very much and felt her sorrow. I really don't think she wanted that to happen but the boys ruled everything around that house. With two brothers in the ministry, I didn't stand a chance. Mom let them make decisions about things and stood by them no matter what.

We headed back to Indiana with Marilynn. The whole episode frightened her and tired me out. I felt ripped to pieces from end to end. I slept for hours on the drive back and Marilynn seemed to calm down. She played with Perry, about the same age.

By the time we got home our moods improved and we enjoyed a great summer. I kept Marilynn for six weeks and we had a great time. I remained at Viola and Charlie's house and went to work as usual. After the episode with my brothers, my nightmares returned. Almost every night I had dreams about Dad and my brothers trying to harm me in some way. Mostly they had guns and knives. I don't know why because they never physically harmed me in any way. Finally, the nightmares stopped.

Marilynn and Perry got along well together, and they played with the neighbor kids as well. I took lots of pictures. My favorite showed one of Marilynn and Perry kissing. She wore a summer dress and big sunglasses. The two of them looked so cute. All too soon the summer ended and the time arrived to take her home.

That huge empty feeling came rushing back and after I dropped her off I quickly got in the car and drove away as fast as I could with tears running down my face. I could hardly see for crying so I pulled off the road and rested for a while. Soon I pulled myself together and then got on my way.

After I got back home everything improved and I felt better again. I called Marilynn every week still, and now she had gotten old enough to talk with me more. That fall Bim and I got back together and decided to have a committed relationship. In September he told me that he planned to work in Texas and wanted me to go there with him. His sister Linda and her two children, Tom and Tabby, planned to go, too, as well as Linda's boyfriend, Kevin. Bim wanted us to get a townhouse and live together. I decided to go. Bim and Kevin went first and found a place to live, then we followed.

Chapter 10

The Move to Texas and Back

I had a silver Chevelle with no radio so I bought some country music magazines that had the words to the songs in them and memorized a lot of songs for the road. The guys left cash for gas money and Linda had all the money. We planned to stop at the same gas stations to fill up. Of course we didn't have cell phones in those days and during the night, Linda and I somehow got separated. I had only a quarter of a tank of gas left and my car burned almost as much oil as it did gas. I heard the engine pinging and knew I had to get some oil before driving any further.

I made it to the Texas line and pulled off at the information center. Stopping next to the pay phones, I got out in the total darkness and made a call to our friend Jessie Shipman, who lived close to the guys. No one had heard from Linda so I told them where I'd stopped and that someone needed to come get me. Being stranded like that scared me to death. I didn't like the darkness and not knowing the whereabouts of my traveling companion. I sat in my car wondering what to do when someone tapped on my window. A man stood there.

He asked me to roll my window down. I refused. He asked me if I needed help.

I said, "No."

He walked away and I watched him get into a semi. He didn't leave and after a half hour came back and asked me again if I needed help. Again I told him no and he left.

When he came back the third time I cracked the window and he said, "I have to go, so if you need me to call someone or if you need to get somewhere I will help you, but I can't help you if you won't let me."

I gave in and told him how I got separated from my traveling companion and so on. He asked me to follow him a few miles down the road to a truck stop. Maybe we'd find Linda there and if not then he'd fill the tank for me and I could follow him as far as Seabrook. Frightened, I agreed to follow him.

We got to the truck stop but I couldn't find Linda. As he promised, he filled my gas tank and filled the oil and then he bought me a cup of coffee. I got his name and address and promised to send him a check and we took off. While at the truck stop I called Jessie to say I'd gotten back on my way.

I followed the truck all the way to my exit. He flashed his lights and then he left. I got a warm feeling all over me; I thought of him as an angel sent to help me. As soon as I could, I sent a check to his address.

Linda and the kids made the trip fine, and we all lived together in a big townhouse. We weren't far from the Gulf and spent lots of time fishing and putting nets in for crabs. I learned to love seafood and enjoyed the ocean.

I hadn't realized before how much Bim, Linda, Kevin,

and their friends loved to smoke marijuana. They smoked and drank beer every evening after work. The kids and I went for walks and hung out. I didn't want them doing drugs and drinking in front of the kids and said as much to Bim.

"Mind your own business, not Linda's."

But I didn't want Bim smoking marijuana either, because I didn't want Marilynn exposed to that if she came to see us or live with us. I told him that, and he assured me he wouldn't do drugs around Marilynn.

We frequented Gilley's and other honkytonks to listen to music, which I loved. I learned how to do the Cotton-eyed Joe.

One day Bim came home and told us about a band named Alabama at Gilley's and we decided to go see them. Soon after we saw them, they got famous and we heard them all over the radio. That evening at Gilley's, Bim casually asked me to marry him. He didn't have a ring but I didn't worry about that. I told him yes and got very excited. I thought most about getting Marilynn back.

As time went on, Bim, Linda, and Kevin got more and more into drugs. They did something every evening. They not only smoked marijuana, but now added a downer they called a "lude." I didn't know what that was but after they smoked a couple of joints, had some beer, and swallowed a lude they lay around like a bunch of dead people. Sometimes they all passed out. I tried to talk to Bim but couldn't catch him at a good time.

We all planned to go see the Rolling Stones at the Astrodome one evening. I told Bim I didn't want to go if he planned to drink and smoke. He promised he'd stay sober. I drove my car because I had a bad feeling about the evening. Riding with them stoned and drunk frightened me. Thirty minutes after we'd gotten there, I couldn't find Bim. I finally found him with glazed eyes. He held a huge beer. When he saw me he dropped his beer and dumped it down his front.

I said, "I'm going home now. You can manage to get home on your own."

He held out his hand and said, "Goodbye, bitch."

I quickly turned around and walked away. I found my car and drove home.

When I got inside I went straight to my closet, got my suitcase out, and packed it. I put it in the car, gathered up all the money I could find and took off for Indiana. I left a note for Bim so he wouldn't worry or go looking for me. I had an uneventful trip to Indiana and it felt good to return to Viola and her family.

After a couple of weeks he called me and apologized over and over. Again he promised to stay away from booze and drugs. I desperately wanted it to work for us because I truly loved him. I decided to give it another try.

In June, Bim came home for a couple of weeks between jobs and I stayed with him at his Dad's house. One evening I couldn't sleep. I couldn't understand why. Nothing I did helped, and when I closed my eyes I could feel them rolling under my eyelids. I tried desperately to relax and fall asleep but nothing worked.

Bim got up and brought me one of his Dad's sleeping pills. I took it and still I could not sleep. Finally, in the early morning hours I thought that something must've happened to someone I knew. When the phone rang at five in the morning, I didn't want to answer.

I heard my brother Chris's voice. He said that my mother had died during the night. He said that they all decided to ban me from the funeral because they felt certain I caused her death. He added that she died exactly five years to the day that I left home.

"She died of colon cancer," I replied.

"No, Emmy, she died because you refused to obey her and Dad," Chris said.

"Chris, I want to come to the funeral."

"No, Emmy, stay away. Unless you wear Amish clothes and plan to stay home, you're not welcome. You're a part of the devil and Mom couldn't bear to see you anymore and that's why she died."

I couldn't talk to Chris anymore so I handed the phone to Bim and left the room.

My heart broke into so many pieces and once again I felt as small and worthless as a piece of dirt. I prayed for help deciding what to do. Then I talked with Viola and she advised me not to go. I didn't.

I spoke with my brother John some time later and he told me the location of Mom's grave. When I went to pick up Marilynn for the summer, we stopped by her grave and planted a rose bush. As always, before leaving, I called ahead and made plans with Marilynn's grandmother.

I arrived right on schedule and found only Carl there. I told him I wanted to pick up Marilynn and he said, "She's with her grandmother and I don't know where."

"Look, she knew I was coming to pick up Marilynn. I'll be back in fifteen minutes."

I left and went immediately to the local sheriff's

department and told them what had transpired. I told them that I didn't trust Carl and feared for my safety. They called Carl and then accompanied me to the house, waiting on the street while I went to get Marilynn. She still wasn't there so the deputy spoke with Carl and he called someone. Marilynn came home and we loaded up and drove straight home.

I took the deputy's advice and left town quickly. We had a safe trip back to Indiana and had a wonderful summer. Marilynn and I spent lots of time together and I felt like we bonded more as she grew older. I put her in swimming lessons and every day we went to Crystal Beach to swim. She grew into a strong swimmer, and getting her out of the water proved difficult. Bim and I lived together again and he behaved himself. He mostly worked out of town all week and came home on weekends.

One weekend he hooked up with his old friend Jessie and they went fishing. At four o'clock in the morning the doorbell rang and there stood Jessie by himself. He told me they'd gotten drunk and got pulled over, and Bim went to jail for driving while intoxicated and possession of marijuana. He told me I'd have to go to the courthouse Monday morning and bail him out. I wanted to leave him there. However, when Monday morning came I got Marilynn ready for swimming lessons then went and bailed out Bim.

The rest of the summer went by quickly and I had to return Marilynn to New York. I had a difficult time dropping her off and driving away. My heart felt empty, and I hurt so much. I cried for miles and miles. Slowly reality sank back in and I got back in the groove of life in

Indiana.

Bim took a job in Port Arthur, Texas, working on a large cooling tower. I stayed in Indiana because I planned to see Marilynn for Thanksgiving. Pam made plans to go up with me. We spoke with our friends who owned the diner and as they planned a trip out of town, they offered their home to us. I loved seeing Marilynn again. She'd turned four years old and had grown so cute. Her short haircut emphasized her little round face and big smile. She welcomed me and I could see her happiness to see me. Pam and I took her shopping for some new clothes. She loved dresses, so we picked out four outfits. She modeled them all for us, posing just like a model, and I took pictures.

For Thanksgiving Day we planned to have dinner with Mr. and Mrs. Tryon, who'd been neighbors of my parents and owned the farm before Mom and Dad bought it. We had a delicious dinner and I very much enjoyed our visit. It felt good so close to my old home, but it also brought me feelings of great sadness for the huge separation between my family and me. I missed my mother every day. After the meal, we said goodbye and headed home.

Marilynn fell asleep in the car on the way home. I carried her into the house and put her to bed, and Pam and I sat down to play cards. She wanted a cold Coke, and I volunteered to go out and get it and immediately got in the car and drove to the Mini Mart on the outskirts of Massena. The parking lot looked deserted and dark, and I noticed a burned-out light. I went in and picked up the drinks.

When I walked outside to my car I went to the passenger side and placed the drinks on the floor.

Suddenly, I felt a very hard cold thing against my neck

and a man's voice said, "Don't say a word and do as I tell you."

I don't remember much after that except seeing a big pile of wood that I walked around. The next thing I remember, I stood on the stairs where Pam and I stayed with Marilynn. I felt dazed and confused. I walked into the house and Pam could see something had happened. I couldn't tell her what, but my torn and dirty clothes gave a clue. Pam wanted to call the police and I wanted to take a bath and get those clothes off immediately.

We called the police and then Pam took me to the emergency room. They treated me very nicely and counseled me for what seemed like hours. The next day more officers visited with me. I went to the site with one of them and I really couldn't see anything or tell where it happened. I couldn't remember anything and didn't want to believe anything happened. Even now I don't remember it all.

I do remember the nurse though. She had brown hair pulled back into a ponytail and big, warm brown eyes. She stayed with me through the whole procedure. The doctors performed several tests and then they cleaned me up and treated me for lacerations and bruising to my vagina. They said I had been raped and gave me helpful information and several hot lines to call if I needed additional help after I left the hospital.

Pam called Bim and he said he'd come get me, which he did, three days later. After Bim arrived, we took Marilynn home. It was a very difficult parting because I didn't know how long it would be before I would see her again.

So many terrible things happened to me up there, I felt lucky to be alive, and sometimes, I wished that I wasn't. I never totally lost my faith in the Lord, but many times I questioned it.

I was very happy to see Bim but also afraid. I didn't know if he'd accept me now. I felt dirty. I felt so violated. But he behaved wonderfully and made getting over it easier for me. He took me to Indiana and left me with Viola.

Still in shock, I didn't realize how negatively the whole thing affected me. By the end of three days I'd lost twelve pounds. I couldn't eat or sleep.

After I returned to Indiana, I stayed indoors all day with the doors locked. I wasn't able to go outdoors by myself. Even when someone went with me, I stopped breathing until I almost passed out. Everything frightened me.

Several weeks later Bim took me back to Port Arthur, Texas, where he still worked. I felt safe with him because he treated me with kindness and caring. However, I still feared leaving the apartment by myself. I tried to talk myself out of these fears and looked out the window or door. I didn't see anything frightening, but as soon as I walked outside, I froze and could not function. I also suffered nightmares, mostly the same dream which started with a monster breaking through the door. In my dreams I tried to jump out of the window but never quite made it. My nightgown always got caught on a nail or something.

After several months I dreamed that I avoided getting caught and successfully jumped to the ground and ran away. I felt so good about the dream that I decided to go to the laundry room that day by myself. I had to go down a flight of stairs then walk across a small lawn and into the laundry room. I refused to think about it too much. Instead, I just got the laundry ready and made a run for it. I thought I could easily run back to the apartment if I wasn't able to get through it.

I tried to stay focused only on getting down the stairs first. When I got to the bottom of the stairs, I thought about going back, then immediately thought about my dream of getting free from the monster. I focused on the laundry room and started across the lawn. I made it to the laundry room, put the clothes in the washer, closed the lid and realized I didn't have money to start the washer! I dropped everything and ran back to the apartment. Exhausted, I rested for a while then went back and completed the task! I felt very proud of myself and felt like I had taken a huge step toward a normal life.

My life improved from then on, but I still had dreams and fears lots of times. I just kept making myself do things, and I got much better. To this day, however, I feel great fear for short periods of time.

During this time, Bim gave me a beautiful diamond ring and asked me again to marry him. I loved him and felt very safe with him, so I said yes. We didn't make any wedding plans at the time but wanted to return to Indiana to marry and make a life. I wanted to go to college now and felt I wanted to be near Viola and her family. We eventually found an apartment in Madison, Indiana.

Bim continued to travel and came to Indiana often to visit. several months later we bought a trailer. Then we found a piece of land in the country to rent. I liked the setting; a barn, several out-buildings, a cornfield in front and big trees in the yard.

I went to Ivy Tech State College in Madison. I got into the medical assistant program and took classes the following semester. I hadn't attended a public school and got very scared at the prospect. I had low self-esteem and felt very shy. But I had lots of determination and told myself over and over that no matter what happened, I intended to stand up straight and keep breathing.

Rain and snow faced me on the first day of class, and I arrived wet and cold. I immediately looked for the bathrooms. I stayed in the bathroom until I saw someone with the same books I had and followed her to the Typing I classroom. She sat down and I took the chair next to her. Whatever she did, I did. I shared a typewriter with her. We went to the same classes and got to be friends. When I conquered my fears, I enjoyed the classes. I made good grades and learned many things.

I saw an ad for a new Arby's and I wanted to earn my own money so I applied. I left with a new job, and planned to work in the evening after I got out of class. Bim continued working out of town and came home as often as he could.

Chapter 11

A Wedding and a New Baby

In May of 1984, Bim and I got married in a little church in Manville, Indiana. A handful of people came to our wedding: Bim's family, Viola and her family, and a few of our friends. We drove to Louisville, Kentucky, and spent the night in a fancy hotel for our honeymoon.

Life went back to normal again. I stayed in touch with Marilynn as much as I could. When she turned six years old, she flew on a plane all by herself. I no longer had to make that long trip up to New York and back. Marilynn didn't mind flying. She followed instructions very well, and showed no fear. I booked her on direct flights so she'd never have to wait in an airport without family. When I picked her up the first time, seeing her walking in from the plane made me cry, partly because of my happiness at seeing her, and partly because I felt so proud of her for her courage and independence. Putting her on the plane home proved the most difficult. It never got easier.

I had little contact with my family. Occasionally I received a letter from someone, mostly to admonish me and to try to convince me to come back to the church. I continued to fight my inner battle with guilt. I often wished I could have a quick talk with God so we could discuss these issues. At times I felt very good about myself and felt confident in my goodness. Then I received a letter, and everything turned the other way.

A couple of times when I felt really bad, I dreamed about my mother. In the dream she appeared happy and she spoke kindly to me. In one dream, she told me how proud she felt of me and hugged me. When I woke up I could still feel where her arms hugged me, and felt certain of her presence. Other times when I felt bad or questioned myself, I talked to Viola. Having grown up Amish, she understood their beliefs and rules.

I finally felt able to let my family members have their say once I understood that I, too, was a child of God. I decided to respect my family's beliefs and knew that each one of them had to continue acting as they had for the church to continue. That's when I let their words roll off my back. I told them I felt sorry for the way I left but said I knew no other way to get free and live my life. I told them I felt like a prisoner and therefore had to sneak out. I also told them that I forgave them for holding me prisoner and understood why they did it. They accepted none of this. They told me they heard only the devil talking. But I felt much more at peace.

I finished the medical assistant program and went to work in a dental office doing administrative duties such as answering the phone, scheduling appointments, billing, and filing insurance. I also made coffee, went on doughnut runs, and ran other errands. I enjoyed my work and soon worked in the back with patients. When we needed another dental assistant, my employer asked me to find my replacement so I could work with the patients. I immediately thought of my friend Robin, also in the medical assistant program. She needed a job and excitedly took the position.

After getting settled in my new job, I talked with Bim about having a baby. I really wanted another baby and also thought it would help me to get custody of Marilynn. Bim didn't really agree or disagree, so I decided to go off the pill. Three months later I got pregnant, and we were both so happy. I felt better than ever during pregnancy, suffering no morning sickness or other ailments. The baby moved around a lot, sometimes turning over and over, at times a little painful.

Bim and I had gone to a cookout with friends when my labor pains began. At first I ignored them because they arrived with irregularity. But soon I changed my mind because of their strength and duration. I told Bim we needed to go to the hospital and he didn't really believe me. He took me home first and I took a quick shower then he wanted me to walk up and down the driveway to see if that made the pain go away. He said he heard somewhere that false labor pains subsided with walking.

He insisted I try this, so I went to the driveway and attempted to walk. The pains felt so intense at times that I lost strength in my legs. He quickly agreed to get me to the hospital. When we arrived they took me in right away. A nurse examined me and then tried to start an IV. My intense pain prevented this. She explained how great pressure from labor pains affected the veins. Finally, after four tries, two in each arm, she sent for another nurse.

Within minutes, a tiny black nurse with a big smile and big dark eyes stood over me and gently placed a needle down through the top of my arm and ended up in an artery. I greatly appreciated her help.

As the nurses hung the medicine to help me with pain, I started giving birth. I truly thought I'd pass out because of the pain. I didn't, and very soon we had a baby girl. I felt excited with my new daughter. The doctor didn't have to spank her to make her breathe. She started screaming the minute she was born. As the doctor measured her, she grew quiet and, with big eyes, looked all around the room. The doctors and nurses all laughed. Even now, our daughter Brooke still likes to hang upside down!

Brooke was a beautiful baby, very alert and perfect in every way. The day after her birth, I realized that she and Dad shared a birth date. I wondered what he'd think if he knew about her. I wondered if he'd want to see her. I hoped so. But when I went to see him and took a picture of Brooke, so he could see that she had the same big blue eyes as his, he showed no interest. He quickly turned the picture upside down, placed it on the table and walked away. He never said a word.

At four weeks old, I took her to the doctor for a checkup. While in the waiting room a little girl wanted to see her and sneezed on her. Soon after the doctor checked her out and pronounced her the picture of health, Brooke got very ill. Bim was away and I rushed her to the hospital because she felt hot to the touch and kept throwing up. I worried about dehydration.

I had to stop several times on the way to the hospital to suction the vomit from her mouth to prevent her from aspirating. We stayed in the emergency room for several hours, then left with lots of instructions. They told me to give her Pedialite for twelve hours then go back to nursing.

When she started nursing she immediately began to throw up again. We went through this several times and finally the doctor advised me to try a milk formula. Brooke didn't like that either and got sick again. My worry grew as she turned listless and lost weight. I expressed my fears to my doctor and he told me to try her on soy milk. If that didn't work. We'd put her in the hospital.

When I introduced the soy milk, Brooke took a very small amount then went to sleep. I watched her every minute. Soon she woke up and I gave her more and she slept again. I began to feel a lot better. She improved with every feeding. She reminded me of a wilted flower coming back to life.

Brooke gained weight and began to smile, and it gave me great pleasure and relief to see her feel better! I couldn't nurse her anymore, but the doctor said since she nursed for the first four weeks, she should have received the most important nutrients for her immune system.

At times like this I greatly missed my mother and sisters. I'd have loved their advice and assistance. I knew I'd sacrifice this when I chose to leave home, but I still cried a lot, especially when Bim wasn't home.

When Brooke turned six weeks old, I went back to work. I begged Bim to let me stay home with her, but he didn't want me to, so I began to look for a babysitter. I heard about an older couple who looked after children. I went to see them and knew immediately this was the place for Brooke. Delphine and Tommy Jett, in their sixties, kept several babies during the day. She agreed to take Brooke and very reluctantly I went back to work.

My boss sent me to Kentucky University to learn how to place fillings and finish them. I enjoyed working in the dental field but thought it would be more interesting to be in the medical field. I applied for a position with a group of heart specialists and began to work with them.

In this position I seated patients and took their history and vital signs in preparation for the doctor. I also assisted with surgical procedures performed in the office.

During this time I received a call from Ivy Tech State College. They needed a secretary for the nursing programs and preferred a medical assistant for that position. They scheduled me for an interview. I felt very good about a position with them, because while going through classes there I made many friendships and grew to love Ivy Tech. It felt like home to me.

Brooke had turned two when I received word from one of my brothers of Dad's illness. He had inoperable cancer and the doctors expected him to live two to four weeks. I called my niece Patti and we drove to see him. He knew about his condition and knew how long he had to live, and I wanted to give him the opportunity to talk to me if he felt he wanted to.

When Patti and I arrived, we found him sitting outdoors in his rocking chair. We walked up to him and I could tell he didn't recognize us. He acted very friendly and after saying hello he talked about the nice weather and so on. Soon my brother Ben walked up and told him our names. Immediately he stopped talking to us and no longer even looked at us. He got up and went indoors. My brother

John also came to spend some time with him. Dad talked with John some, but not me.

We stayed three days and during that time John and I had some time to get to know each other a little better. John hadn't gotten baptized in the church so they weren't required to excommunicate him from the church. He didn't know that the church had excommunicated me, and felt stunned when they didn't allow me to sit at the table and eat with the rest of the family.

When Patti told him, he told me that he'd prevent this treatment from going on. John spoke to Ben and called it cruel treatment. He said if the family couldn't eat with me, then they shouldn't eat with him either because we live the same kind of lives. I felt very happy to get this kind of support from my brother.

The treatment continued. John sat with me in the back of the room and ate with me instead of sitting at the table with the family.

During my time there I tried to spend as much time near Dad as possible. When I tried to help him with his shoes he pushed me away with his arm and he never again talked to me until I prepared to leave. Still, I believe deep down he felt happy to see me and that in some way he felt some kind of love for me.

Exactly two weeks later he died and I went back for the funeral. John and I stayed in the same hotel and met for breakfast the morning of the funeral. I saw a couple, dressed in black, having breakfast not far from us. I wondered if they also planned to go to the funeral. As soon as I walked in the house I saw that couple and they saw me. The woman introduced herself and I met my cousins on

Dad's side, Jim and Karon Schwartz, also non-Amish. I felt great pleasure to meet them. We stayed in touch and I certainly have enjoyed them.

As we filed by the casket and took our last look at Dad's body, I felt sad that we never had a loving relationship. I felt even a greater sadness that he felt he'd lived his life the right way by shutting me out. After the service, the boys loaded the casket into the big top buggy and drove to the little graveyard where they buried Mom. My sister Lydia, who had a four-week-old baby boy, made the trip to upstate New York from Pennsylvania in the back of a pickup truck on a mattress. She attended the graveside service. Lydia and I stood together as the boys buried Dad in a grave next to Mom. I enjoyed seeing the family and visiting with nieces, nephews, and cousins. I had some pleasant visits, mostly from some of my old students, but my cousins and immediate family continued to admonish me for my way of life.

Chapter 12

More Changes

As Marilynn grew older, she repeatedly said she wanted to live with us. On several occasions she asked her father, who always said no. After Brooke arrived, Marilynn asked again. I talked with her about it and asked her if she could tell her father how she felt. She always told me that she could not. At ten years old, she visited us and cried almost every evening during her last week with us. She said she really wanted me to do something so she could stay. So I called her father and told him of her constant requests. He asked to speak with her. When I put her on the phone, he asked her if she felt okay about returning home and she said yes. I knew then that she needed to stand up for what she wanted, and that I couldn't get custody until she did.

When Marilynn turned twelve, she changed. Older and more mature, she really knew what she wanted. Marilynn and I talked about her living with us, then we talked with Bim. We all agreed to try to regain custody. When I made the first appointment with our attorney, Bim didn't show up and I went ahead on my own. I had a deep, sinking feeling about his absence. He'd not prevented me from filing for custody, but I knew about his feelings of having more responsibility and another child around the house. He went back to using the alcohol and drugs. When he drank, he turned mean and ugly. Sometimes he threw me around, but mostly he yelled and used very foul language.

I went forward on my own with the custody case. I made a black suit for myself and a dress for Marilynn and we headed for New York. Going there terrified me, and we stayed in different hotels every night. I paid in cash and never used my own name.

Marilynn and I met with our attorneys and after a few days in court, I won custody and we returned home. I finally felt complete with my little family.

That fall, both girls got all dressed up for the first day of school and I watched them get on the bus with a joyful heart. However, Bim and I felt unhappy. We talked about it but he didn't reveal much to me. Actions always speak louder than words, and he spent less and less time at home, fell asleep on the couch more, and got meaner and more violent at times. We divorced, and the girls and I stayed in the house in town and he moved out to our farm.

I continued to work at Ivy Tech and got accepted into the nursing program at night. It made for very long days for us, but after two years I had my nursing degree and I knew as long as I could work, I could take care of my girls.

When Marilynn went to Florida on her senior trip, Brooke and I went to Disneyland. In California we visited friends of mine who lived in the Santa Ynez Valley. I really fell in love with the valley, and when Marilynn graduated from high school, I put the house up for sale and thought if it sold quickly, I'd move to California. The house sold in the first month and we loaded up a big U-Haul and moved. I got a job working with a group of internal medicine specialists and stayed with them for three years, then went into home health care. I enjoyed the area very much.

After Marilynn finished college, she came to live with me. In 2002 we decided to move to the live music capital…Austin, Texas. Brooke now lives in Indiana with her father. She has a large family on his side and loves the area. Brooke has a beautiful baby daughter, Alexis, the apple of my eye. We visit each other often.

I continue to miss my family and at times experience great sadness for the separation. I have, however, a great feeling of peace and know and understand myself more than ever now. I know that the Lord is my Shepherd and He leads me in my life. Sometimes I travel rough roads but it makes the smooth parts better. I love my girls and enjoy my friends, music, dancing, good food, and I look forward to the future.

To order additional copies of
Daring Destiny

Name _____

Address _____

_____

_____

$14.95 x _____ copies =   _____

Sales Tax   _____
(Texas residents add 8.25% sales tax)

Please add $3.50 postage and handling   _____

Total amount due: _____

Please send check or money order for books to:

Special Delivery Books
WordWright Business Park
46561 SH 118
Alpine, TX 79830

For a complete catalog of books,
visit our site at
http://www.SpecialDeliveryBooks.com

Printed in the United States
66141LVS00001B/63

9 781932 196795